My Letters...

M.K. Gandhi

*Edited by:* Prof. Prasoon

*Cedar books*

*Published by:*

*Cedar books*

*An Imprint of*
**Pustak Mahal**®, Delhi
J-3/16, Daryaganj, New Delhi-110002
☎ 23276539, 23272783, 23272784 • *Fax:* 011-23260518
*E-mail:* info@pustakmahal.com • *Website:* www.pustakmahal.com

**Sale Centre**
- 10-B, Netaji Subhash Marg, Daryaganj, New Delhi-110002
  ☎ 23268292, 23268293, 23279900 • *Fax:* 011-23280567
  *E-mail:* rapidexdelhi@indiatimes.com
- **Hind Pustak Bhawan**
  6686, Khari Baoli, Delhi-110006
  ☎ 23944314, 23911979

**Branches**
**Bengaluru:** ☎ 080-22234025 • *Telefax:* 080-22240209
*E-mail:* pustak@airtelmail.in • pustak@sancharnet.in
**Mumbai:** ☎ 022-22010941, 022-22053387
*E-mail:* rapidex@bom5.vsnl.net.in
**Patna:** ☎ 0612-3294193 • *Telefax:* 0612-2302719
*E-mail:* rapidexptn@rediffmail.com
**Hyderabad:** *Telefax:* 040-24737290
*E-mail:* pustakmahalhyd@yahoo.co.in

© Publisher
**Edition: 2010**
ISBN 978-81-223-1109-9

Printed at : Param Offsetters, Okhla, New Delhi-110020

# Preface

One day, when I met Shri Rohit Kumar Gupta, Director Pustak Mahal, in his office, straightaway he offered me to collect and edit the letters of Mahatma Gandhi. With it he took off his right hand from his lap and I noticed *"My Experiments With Truth"* and also his index finger in the book. Obviously, he was reading the book.

It was his contention that it would be a service to the general readers to make the important letters written by Mahatma Gandhi, available to them. It will give insight into the mind, personality, approach, attitude and planning of Bapu. His ideas and ideals can be put to better use by the people as they are relevant and essential for terror-stricken, unstable world.

Then, we discussed and finalised which letters, what type of letters and letters addressed to whom, are to be collected and compiled.

After a week started the book-fair and he bought many needed books for me. Yet, I had to consult *"Complete Works of Mahatma Gandhi"* from where all these letters are taken.

The letters included in **"My Letters"** show the true self of the Mahatma, his pragmatic ways and spiritual strength. It is better to read the letters and understand his philosophy. There is no need to imitate him but one must follow him, imbibe and make his ideas, ideals and qualities own guide; and try intelligently and diligently to make the mother earth a better and peaceful place for all beings. With this open intention **"My Letters"** is now in the hands of readers

At the most needed places **ā** has been used for longer 'a' sound.

**Prof. Shrikant Prasoon**
Solomon Complex
Motihari; Champaran
*Mobile:* 09868082133
*e-mail:* shrikantprasoon@yahoo.co.in
*web:* www.shrikantprasoon.com

# Contents

**SECTION-I**

**Gandhi Re-introduced**

The Need for Re-introduction  9
Pragmatic Gandhian Philosophy  13
Gandhi: An Attached and Detached Personality  20
Important Events in the Life of Mahatma Gandhi  24
Imprisonments of Mahatma Gandhi  26
Fasts Observed by Mahatma Gandhi  27
The Letters  29

**SECTION-II**

**Selected But Complete Letters**

*Letters to...*    Moti Lal Nehru  35
Jawahar Lal Nehru  43
Vallabh Bhai Patel  81
M.A. Jinnah  112
Lord Mountbatten  133
Lord Wavell  148
Lord Irwin  153
The Viceroy  159
Mira Behn  161
Adolf Hitler  168
Subhash Chandra Bose  173
Sarojini Naidu  180
C. Raja Gopalachari  186
G. D. Birla  197
Rabindra Nath Tagore  205
F. D. Roosevelt  208
S. Radhakrishnan  212
Jaiprakash Narayan  216
Prabhavati  228
Rajendra Prasad  229
J. B. Kripalani  232
Kasturba Gandhi  236

SECTION-I

Gandhi Re-introduced

# The Need for Re-introduction

Mahatma Gandhi is in every city, village and home, then what is the need for re-introducing Gandhi. Actually, it is very essential to re-introduce Gandhi because either we have hung Gandhi by the walls or shut him in the shelves or almirah as printed words. Gandhi is not in us, not in our thought and never in action. Both our thinking and actions have become unlike that of Gandhi; almost anti-Gandhi. So, there is a need to re-introduce the Mahatma.

Now, the whole of Gandhi is before us: his life; words; deeds and accomplishments; but we are unable to show or see the whole of him. Even this book contains only his selected letters, a small part of his writing, only a few hundred out of the thousands of letters that he wrote.

We are partly reading Gandhi and analysing only a part of it and him, and like modernity, touching and feeling only parts and living only in parts. So, it is a simple, and of course, a partial attempt to re-introduce Gandhi, an effort to see the whole of him, which eludes us. The illusion is within and with us. Gandhi had no illusions. His letters will amply show the clarity in his visions, assertions and statements. This proves amply that Gandhi was a Mahatma, Mahā Ātmā, a great soul, known as the Mahatma or Bapu or Rashtrapita. He possessed a great soul which showed in everything that he did, said or wrote; in his approach and attitude towards life, his behaviour with one and all, and his acceptance of many incidents and in true expression of thought.

Some selfish and arrogant persons tried to demean him, but failed miserably because of Gandhi's purity and also because of the fact that Gandhi's greatness is real. There was neither a cover nor he ever tried to cover anything. He denounced each wrong deed and each mental or physical attack and went on fast for others' immoral acts. He punished others by punishing himself, he attacked without actually attacking and without using a weapon. (Non-violence is often declared to be his weapon while non-violence protects all, and kills none. Hence, it is never a weapon, and Gandhi did not use it as a weapon, though even in this re-introduction, it is called his weapon.)

Gandhi's greatness, plainness and simplicity can neither be exaggerated nor surpassed. In all these three aspects, he was at the extreme ends or the highest peaks. Some have tried to iconise him but failed because Gandhi was far greater than what they were able to project, show or describe. It is always difficult to accurately describe that, which is plainly visible, simple and without artificial colour or cover. Gandhi was, Gandhi is and Gandhi will remain because of his control over and balance between words and deeds.

When Gandhi was killed, he was not hurt, not in the least. On the contrary, the life was hurt, the people were hurt, the world was hurt. The whole world is still bleeding. Terror is reaching new heights, depth and width. It's three dimensional growth for terror and crime. It is growing at a faster speed; killing embryo, children, young, grown-up, old, workers, businessmen, soldiers and officers without discrimination. It is indiscriminate killing of all living beings, particulary human beings. It is the aftereffect of the killing of Gandhi, a Mahatma, which is a declaration that arms will be freely and frequently used against un-armed, innocent and harmless people.

All are making some mistakes somethere. In place of reading and thinking absurd stuff, Gandhi must be read, understood and followed for a fearless, healthy, peaceful and prosperous co-existence. It is essential to avoid attack by one community on another, by Australians on Indians, by Marathis on Biharis etc.

That is why it is essential to re-introduce Gandhi. It must be clear and clearly stated and accepted that Gandhi did not die. Mahatma's like Gandhi never die. Gandhi is alive, his methods are more effective. Each one should make him, his ideas and ideals, his words and deeds, part and parcel of one's self, words, goals, ideals and actions. One must activate the Gandhian philosophy inside and project it to others as example by following that living idol, and his saviour philosophy so that life and living beings are not wasted for financial and material gain. Destruction is always fatal both for destroyers and the destroyed. Believe it, 73 million kilometres' hole in the Ozone layer is fatal for all; MSDs and Nuclear weapons, including its garbage will annihilate. Remember, all the killers have already been killed. Killers and lustful live in fear and die unceremoniously. Gandhi must be re-introduced to all, and Gandhian philosophy must be followed both for immediate relief and resurrection.

Gandhi is not a corporeal body but a worldly and divine idea, common emotion, uncommon faith, mass-hope and en-mass dynamism.

Gandhi is truth and insistence on truth, he experimented with truth, made truth his active and effective instrument and defeated the most powerful rule and army of the time.

Gandhi was co-operative. He co-operated with all, including the ruler and Viceroy, as  a contrast he started and led Non-cooperation Movements to achieve the nation's cherished goal.

Gandhi was lean and thin but neither unhealthy nor weak. He proved himself to be the most powerful person of his time with his unseen strength, ungauged energy and indomitable spirit

Gandhi is great when seen though competent eyes or prejudiced eyes; analysed, portrayed and presented by an intelligent or balanced mind or an ignorant one. Many can surpass Gandhi in this or that field but none can even be compared to him when the whole, all the aspects and facets, is presented together. One must see Gandhi from holistic point of view. Gandhi is the whole, not in parts, though, even the parts illumine and illuminate.

Don't imitate Gandhi but follow him; imbibe his qualities: determination, dedication, devotion, confidence, fearlessness, truthfulness, non-violence, tolerance, insistence, compassion, co-operation and guidance by example. Gandhi was all practice, hardly a theory. Don't preach or praise but practise Gandhism.

□

# Pragmatic Gandhian Philosophy

Gandhi said or wrote only that which was clear, clean, true and healthy in his eyes, which his conscience allowed and which he followed himself. His statements had the power to improve broken, scattered, withered, suppressed and suffering Indian society; to take the pain away by curing the centuries old ailments, to save people from falling apart by uniting and re-strengthening them, and were capable of fostering and rejuvenating people. It made him a saviour as it awakened the whole nation and freed it.

The people needed faith and confidence, he became an emblem of both. He did not pour it from outside. He made people aware of the immence strength and power that was hidden and dormant in them. He said that the final aggregate of all the living beings is God. The totality is God. We may not be gods but we have emanated from the God. We are a part of the God, similar to a drop which is a part of the ocean and represents it. If and when a drop is dirty, it does not mean that the whole oceean is dirty. Humanity is the ocean and each man is like a drop of humanity:

*"The sum to that of all that lives is God. We may not be God, but we are of God, even as a little drop of water is of the ocean. You must not lose faith in humanity. Humanity is an ocean, if four-drops of the ocean are dirty, the ocean does not become dirty."*

It is correct that a few drops will not make the ocean dirty but the drops, the individual should also be clean. The cleanliness of the individuals will immensely enhance the value and effect of human beings, and the humanity on a whole. Ethical living and strong moral character will keep every thing clean and pure. For it, Gandhi laid stress on four things: **Truth; Non-violence; Frugality;** and **Plain-living.** These four **sutras** or **Mantras** are essential for all, only then natural and fuller living is possible.

In Gandhian philosophy or Gandhi's way of life, there is no space or existence for rich and poor, high and low, caste or creed. All are human and equal. Human qualities are for each human being; and we need them earnestly for existence and sustenance.

Wherever Gandhi went, and they were numerous, he cleaned the place, people and their mind. On the contrary, at the present, we are making everything, every place, person and mind dirty and contaminated, including the environment and atmosphare particularly the topmost layer; the exosphere. Strangely enough, we are doing it in the name or pretext of cleaning them. Naturally, human existence and the human abode, the earth is in danger.

Only they fall that opt and endeavour for grandeur. They are not healthy and they fail to enjoy life. They fail to achieve a balance between personal aspiration, family and social needs and wholesome human deeds. They need security and are forced to construct a den and shut themselves inside it. They are aggrieved. They suffer, they are restless. They live away from 'life'. It is an unpleasant life full of fears and apprehensions. They carry and spread fear. Life is not improved by degenerating into luxurious living in a material den. It becomes a bliss with pure, wholesome deeds through a plain and simple life.

Gandhi lived and taught a simple, plain life. His ideas became a philosophy of peace and progress during his life time. His philosophy got established as *Gandhivād*, Gandhism in a very natural way. The soul of his philosophy is incessant refinement and progress. It is like an eternal source of energy. It always flows, cleans, makes dutiful, keeps busy in constructive works and thus gives both *health* and *happiness*.

**There are eleven fundamental facts of Gandhism:**

1. Truth *(Satya)*

2. Non-violence *(Ahimsā)*

3. Overall Progress in 7 'Ss' :

    i. *Swāsthya (health)*

    ii. *Sampati (wealth)*

    iii. *Sāhitya (literature and study)*

    iv. *Sabhyatā (civilisation)*

    v. *Samskriti (Culture)*

    vi. *Sadbuddhi (Higher intellect) and*

    vii. *Sadbhāvanā (compassion)*

4. Simple Living (*Sādagi*)

5. Control (*Sanyam*)

6. Equality (*Rāma-Rājya*)

7. Traditional Profession (*Vanshānugat Uddyam*)

8. Physical Labour (*Shāririka Shram*)

9. Decentralisation (*Vikendrikaran*)

10. Local Self Government (*Grām Panchayat*) and

11. Cottage Industry (*Kutir Udyog*)

Man is no longer human because of excessive materialism, exuberant luxury and growing ego caused by science and technical inventions. For it and through it, man is bent upon misuse and destruction. Because of the ego, man has forgotten that only 'Nature' can give and save life.

Gandhian philosophy brings man closer to 'Nature' and natural living, away from the artificiality. It teaches man to be cultured and refined than accumulator of extravagant cult and wealth. It aims at equality. It treats all to be equal and gives equal opportunity to all. Modern man talks of equality but won't tolerate it, while tolerance is a natural outcome of non-violence, the basis of Gandhian philosophy.

Gandhi wanted the cottage industry to grow, to give enough work to each hand as an answer to unemployment and idleness. But modern man is dependent on heavy machinery which need electrical energy and produce a lot of similar things in less time. The products are not consumed within the given time. So, people are forced to use expired medicines, food articles, drinks at the heavy cost of their health. Moreover, the garbage coming out of the concerned factories is poison: instant death for small creature but prolonged illness and pain for human beings, and hazardous pollution for earth, water, air, atmosphere and plants. People are vying for a lot of products and immediate and immense gain. On the contrary, Gandhi wanted work, health, simplicity and happiness.

In order to avoid misuse of natural wealth, and pollution, and to feed the growing population each hand needs work and needs to work. The answer is the ways of Gandhi: *Simplicity, Plainness, Tolerance* and *Diligence.*

The worst things that the factories are manufacturing are different types of automatic guns and weapons of mass destruction. Disarmament is the greatest need as an answer to growing use of arms and ammunitions and terrorism. Man will use weapons if he possesses them. If and when the weapons are not there, only then man can be or remain non-violent.

Gandhism can teach love and compassion to the world, give energy, confidence and fearlessness, make life safe and keep freedom intact. It can guarantee the continuity of life on the mother earth, the only planet that has life. Only Gandhism can pragmatically and smoothly solve the problems of the world: of life in general and of human beings in particular.

But Gandhi and Gandhism is knowingly and deliberately being discarded. In place of trying to fight alone with the fast spreading maladies, it is better to adopt the philosophy of Gandhi and make combined effort to wipe out the maladies in time to avoid extinction of life from the earth, which is not possible by searching and escaping to other life-friendly planets.

Most of the people have not seen Gandhi, or read him. Many have failed to understand Gandhi after reading, but greater is the number of such people that have read only a small part of the prolific writer. There are only a fistful people that truly recognise the power and impact of Gandhi. Even among them, there are the blind followers of Gandhi that have nothing to do with logic and reason, and the other is the group of persons that have become like Gandhi, live, work and perform deeds like the Mahatma.

They are the true followers of Gandhi: intelligent, diligent, tolerant and compassionate. They are the persons that must come forward and lead the nation and the world, and spread the philosophy, doctrines and principles of Gandhi to give security and ensure continuity to the living beings. They can make the world a happy heaven.

Those, that have not seen Gandhi, take him to be ineffective. Those, that have not read Gandhi, think him to be irrelevant and out of contest. Those, that have not understood Gandhi, hover and at times oppose him but mostly support him. Those, that have known, read and understood Gandhi, follow Gandhi and lead a very healthy, peaceful and serene life. They are satisfied, and hence, don't take the trouble of making a better world, create better environment for the safety, security and growth of others.

They are inactive. They have forgotten that Gandhi opposed 'inaction and idleness'. He preferred work and diligence. As a result, all see, feel and suffer at the hands of crime, criminals, terrorism and terrorist. They are only idle spectators. When asked, they repeat the stereotyped oft-repeated dialogue as answer, "What can we do?" It is the language of the weak, not of Gandhi or a Gandhian.

Gandhi was not weak. Gandhism preaches opposing the strongest, wrong-deeds in a peaceful, non-violent way. We are accepting all excesses, opposing none, hence suffering a lot. It is not a pure, wholesome and moral life, if the intentions are not good, if human values are ignored and if injustice and crimes are being silently tolerated.

The effect of everything modern invention (from junk food to electronic gadgets) is physical i.e. mental illness, pollution and annihilation, so, Gandhi and Gandhian pilosophy is really relevant and needed for health, peace, security and prosperity. All are restless, unhealthy, unhappy, all are somehow pulling on without hope, without faith and without a respite in view.

Killing human beings has become a part of everyday life and happening of every city. No one can calculate how many unnatural deaths occurred during one year. People feel no pain even at 'mass murders.' Love, pity, sympathy, compassion are alien to modern man but these are the strength of Gandhian diction.

These are the important reasons that we need Gandhi, Gandhian philosophy and must follow Gandhian way of life. Gandhism keeps everything under control, pacifies and restores peace. Follow Gandhi with confidence and dedication for a better and secure future.

We need to know Gandhi, as a symbol and as an 'ism'; and follow him with open eyes and mind, with the global view, keeping the welfare of all human beings in mind.

Gandhism is unemotional but it raises heavy currents and torrents of emotions. It is un-reasoned 'ism', spontaneous and personal that was examined, analysed, explained and synthesised everywhere and is being analysed, explained and followed 'world over'.

Gandhism is based on the plain life, behaviour, deeds and words of Gandhi, on the truth that he experimented with, the non-violence and non-co-operation that he advocated, preached and vehemently used at different time, places and contexts throughout his life. Gandhism is and was lived in practical, day-today life; and it became the life-force that led India to freedom. That force remained active even after his departure and guided India to emerge as the biggest democracy of the world, and a power to reckon with. It has definitely played a vital and effective role in the formation, existence, growth and rise of modern free India. It is clear that it can be equally effective in keeping war-mongers, terrorists and criminals in check, and with its positive values and its longing for natural setting and life, it can create a peacful, safe world for life to sustain and continue.

❑

# Gandhi: An Attached and Detached Personality

Gandhi was a completely attached and really detached person. He did everything from the core of his heart; fully dedicated and deeply engrossed in the things that he did. He was either decidedly assured of the result or was aloof, disinterested and detached from the effects. Come what may, he did whatever his conscience allowed him to do; he protested against and disobeyed what was not acceptable to his conscience. He was not affected or deterred by the results. He was a living example of *Sakām Kartā* and *Niskām Bhoktā*.

Detachment or attachment, the perception, thought and actions of Gandhi were caused not only by social needs or political silence but also because of spiritual attainments. No one can be a Mahatma, great soul, in India with only social and political accomplishments, spiritual and inner growth is essential. His spiritual thinking, pious living, clear vision, unveiling truth and intense faith turned him into a Mahatma. It was the natural outcome of his multi-demensional life, character, personality and spontaneous simple actions and reactions. One can't be a Mahatma with single track thinking and movement.

The attached and detached life and personality of Gandhi can be expressed in different words and even through opposite meanings.

Gandhi was a worker, co-ordinator, organiser: confident, dedicated and determined person. He symbolised actions: detached but purposeful; complete and resolute. He was the central object: able to organise and establish; safe and conscious that gave others safety and awakened all that came in contact.

Gandhi was an idea and purpose, the idea for those who lacked everything and purpose for those who possessed everything. He was the idea of pursuit and purpose behind the pursuit.

Gandhi was a concept: instant and temporal, working and workable, full of passion and also without emotion. He was such a temporary concept that changed into an eternal deathless concept during his life time.

Gandhi was energy: creative, analytical and synthetic. He was the power and energy of both the weak and strong, and became their messiah, protector and saviour.

Gandhi was the mouth, the mouthpiece and the sound: he was the vibrating and echoing sound of millions of people, represented millions of them and spoke through millions of mouths.

Gandhijee was the dream of all the Indians and one that changed the dreams into reality. He never lived in dreams or dreamy milieu. He moved on solid soil with a strong base, and so success either moved along with him or followed him.

Gandhi was a devotee and instrument; an accomplisher and finisher. He was a purifier; a person who took the obstacles away, gave correct solutions, laid ways and kept them clear for others to march ahead safely behind him.

Gandhi was and had a halo: illumined and illuminating, full of vitality and force. He kept the brightness intact. He was himself a proof: authentic and balanced.

21

Gandhi was both a *Karma Yogi* and *Bhāva Yogi:* one that was able to transform each idea into action. His socialistic impulses were his devotion, resurrection of the nation was his only desire, and freedom was the goal. There was a continuity, stability, durability and perpetuity in his ideas, concepts and actions.

Gandhi was an inspiration, an impetus, one that inspired a multitude in a moment: both with presence and words. Though, he was a traveller, he became a path, an inn on long and tiring difficult way and also a guide to take the followers up to safe shore.

Gandhi was himself an indomitable entity: free, definite, micro and macro, immeasurable; that made others free from anxieties and worries. He was a domainless entity that gave domain to others; added essence to others and turned them into essential. He was the entity that became strength of others.

Gandhi was a weapon: a sharp double-edged weapon; automatic and effective; a rare and powerful weapon but non-violent weapon; a weapon that illumined the truth and wiped out falsehood and impurities. He was a quality who praised, enhanced and utilised the qualities of others, he added qualities and increased the value of existing qualities.

Gandhi usually remained quiet, kept others quiet and pacified. He loved and liked peace. Non-violence was his strength and non-cooperation was his favourite simple or difficult path.

Gandhi was a substitute to the desires and wishes of all others, but there was no substitute to Gandhi. There is no substitute to Gandhi even now.

It is apparent and true that there are some integral oppositions in the ideas and actions, philosophy and deeds of Gandhi but he absorbed them well and completely. It is another well known truth that Gandhi preferred co-operation, opted and asked for co-operation but started non-cooperation movement to accomplish the purpose.

Gandhi fought. He was always at the centrestage of struggle. He remained active in struggle throughout his life; led the movement for freedom. He was the commander but he was always far away from violence. He won freedom through non-violence, he sowed the seeds of non-violent ideas and movements and gave the final and perfected produce to the world.

There is no doubt that Gandhi gave power and energy to all but it is also true that he assimilated and absorbed the power of others and grew stronger. Millions and millions of Indians were his power. Whatever he said, the whole nation repeated, wherever he turned, the whole nation turned behind him. People loved, respected, adored and obeyed him. That is the real reason that Gandhi is still living as an idea and dictum, a *sutra* or aphorism, and Gandhism is known and established truth.

To give and absorb the power and to become energetic, active and illumined is Gandhism. One must help the weak but one should never grow weak. There should not be any weakness neither inside nor outside, neither in self nor in action. To win over the weaknesses is Gandhism.

It is a tribute and obeisance to the great and perfact soul, Mahatma Gandhi.

Jai Gandhi!

□

# Important Events in the life of Mahatma Gandhi

| | |
|---|---|
| 02.10.1869 | Birth in Porbandar; a part of Kāthiabāda state; in a Vaishya family; Grandfather was a Deewān. Parents : Karamchand Gandhi and Putali Bai. and Impact of **Shravana** and **Harishchandra.** |
| May, 1883 | Married to Kastur Bā when a student in a High school. They had four sons Hari Lal born in 1888; Mani Lal born in 1892; Rāmdās born in 1897; Devadas born in 1900. |
| 04.09.1888 | Went to Southempton at the age of 18 to become a barrister. |
| 10.06.1891 | Returned to India after passing the Law Exam. Got the sad news of demise of his mother. started Law practice in Mumbai. |
| April, 1893 | Went to Africa at the invitation of Abdullāh and Co., Durban. After a week went to Pretoria. |
| November, 1896 | Went to Natal and returned back to Durban along with wife and children. |
| 1901 | Returned back to India, Met Gokhale, travelled throughout India. |
| 1908 | Went to Africa. |
| 1893-1914 | Civil Rights Movement in South Africa. |
| January, 1915 | Returned to India, established Āshram. Begins his struggle for Indian Independence. Met Gopāl Krishna Gokhale; joined and addressed Indian National Congress. |
| Febraury, 1916 | Went to Benares Hindu University. |
| 15 April, 1917 | Visit to Champaran, started Kisān Movement, established Basic Schools. |

| | |
|---|---|
| April, 1918 | Gandhi supported the empire during World War I and agreed to help recruit Indians for the war. Gandhi's **Champāran** *Satyāgraha* and *Kisān Āndolan*. |
| 13 April, 1919 | Jaliānwāllā Bāgha, Gandhi kept fast for three days, announced that 5,200 died and 3,600 were injured. |
| December, 1921 | Reorganised Congress, *Swarāj was declared to be the goal.* |
| Febrauary, 1922 | Chauri Chaurā, Gandhi observed fast. |
| 31.12.1929 | Demand for '*Purna Swarājya*'. |
| 12.03.1930 | Dandi Yatra (21 Miles); Salt *Satyāgraha, Namak Āndolan* came to an end when he prepared salt at **Dāndi**. India's Independence Day celebrated in Lāhore. |
| 06.04.1930 | Prepared salt |
| November, 1930 | First Round Table Conference |
| 05.03.1931 | Gandhi-Irwin Pact |
| 29.08.1931 | Went to participate in $2^{nd}$ Round Table Conference |
| 1936 | Lucknow session of the Congress |
| 09.08.1942 | Quit India Movement, Arrested |
| 10.02.1943 | Fasting in Āgā Khān Palace Prison |
| February, 1944 | Death of Kasturba Gandhi |
| 1945 | Election |
| 12.08.1946 | Nehru invited to form an Indian Government; Jinnah announced Direct Action Day |
| 6 October, 1946 | Opposed the partition of India to create Pakistan, in the Harijan. |
| | "They can cut me to pieces but they can't make me subscribe to something which I considered to be wrong." |

| May 1947 | Called to Delhi |
| 15.08.1947 | Partition and Freedom |
| 30.01.1948 | Killed by Nāthu Rām Godse in Birla Bhawan. |

□

# Imprisonments of Mahatma Gandhi

## In South Africa

| S.N. | Date of Arrest | Date of Release | Place |
|------|----------------|-----------------|-------|
| 1. | 10-01-1908 | 30-01-1908 | Johannesburg |
| 2. | 07-10-1908 | 25-10-1908 | Volksrust |
| 3. | 26-10-1908 | 05-11-1908 | Johannesburg |
| 4. | 06-11-1908 | 12-12-1908 | Volksrust |
| 5. | 25-02-1909 | 02-03-1909 | Volksrust |
| 6. | 03-03-1909 | 24-05-1909 | Pretoria |
| 7. | 06-11-1913 | 07-11-1913 | Charlestown |
| 8. | 09-11-1913 | 12-11-1913 | Dundee |
| 9. | 12-11-1913 | 17-11-1913 | Volksrust |
| 10. | 18-11-1913 | 17-12-1913 | Bloemfontein |

## In India

| S.N. | Date of Arrest | Date of Release | Place |
|------|----------------|-----------------|-------|
| 1. | 09-04-1919 | 11-04-1919 | Railway Carriage |
| 2. | 13-03-1922 | 20-03-1922 | Sabarmati Jail |
| 3. | 21-03-1922 | 11-01-1924 | Yervada jail |
| 4. | 12-01-1924 | 05-02-1924 | Yervada jail |
| 5. | 05-05-1930 | 26-01-1931 | Yervada jail |
| 6. | 04-01-1932 | 08-05-1933 | Yervada jail |
| 7. | 01-08-1933 | Released for-shifting | Sabarmati Jail |
| 8. | 02-08-1933 | 04-08-1933 | Yervada jail |
| 9. | 04-08-1933 | 23-08-1933 | Yervada jail |
| 10. | 09-08-1942 | 06-05-1944 | Aga Khan Palace Prison, Poone. |

□

# Fasts Observed by Mahatma Gandhi

| S.N. | Date | Place | Reason for Fasting |
|------|------|-------|--------------------|
| 01. | 01-06-1915 | Ahmedabad | Falsehood among Ashram Boys. |
| 02. | 11-09-1915 | Ahmedabad | Against objections to a Harijan. |
| 03. | 12-09-1915 | Ahmedabad | Smoking by an Ashramvasi. |
| 04. | 12 to 15-06-1916 | Ahmedabad | Manilal had sent money to Harilal. |
| 05. | 15 to 17-03-1918 | Ahmedabad | For the wages of mill-hands. |
| 06. | 06-04-1919 | Mumbai | Started Ist Satyagraha with a fast. Observed fast on 6th April every year. |
| 07. | 13-04-1919 | Ahmedabad | Jailianwalla bagh Massacre. Observed fast on this day every year. |
| 08. | 13 to 15-04-1919 | Ahmedabad | Riots at Mumbai, Ahmedabad etc. |
| 09. | 19 to 21-11-1921 | Mumbai | Disturbances in Mumbai caused by the visit of Prince of Wales. |
| 10. | 28-11-21, Monday | Ahmedabad | Disturbances in Mumbai. Kept fast from that day, on every Monday, all his life. |
| 11. | 12 to 16-02-1922 | Bardoli | Massacre at Chauri Chaurā. |
| 12. | 17 to 30-09-1924 | Delhi | For Hindu-Muslim Unity. |
| 13. | 01 to 07-10-1924 | Delhi | For Hindu-Muslim Unity. |
| 14. | 24 to 30-11-1925 | Ahmedabad | Misdeed by boys and girls of the Ashram. |
| 15. | 22 to 24-06-1928 | Ahmedabad | Some immoral act by an Ashramvasi. |

| 16. | 20 to 25-09-1932 | Yervada Jail | Against some decision by the Prime Minister of Britain. |
|---|---|---|---|
| 17. | 03-12-1932 | Yervada | To protest against the Government's decision. |
| 18. | 08 to 28-05-1933 | Parnakuti Poone | For self-purification |
| 19. | 16 to 22-05-1933 | Yervada Jail | In protest against the Government. |
| 20. | 07 to 13-08-1934 | Wardha | For injury to Pandit Lalnath. |
| 21. | 03 to 06-03-1939 | Rajkot | Against the Rajkot Ruler. |
| 22. | 12 to 13-11-1940 | Sevagram | Theft by an Ashramvasi. |
| 23. | 25 to 27 -04-1941 | Sevagram | Riots in Mumbai and Ahmedabad. |
| 24. | 29-06-1941 | Sevagram | For communal harmony |
| 25. | 10-02-1943 to 02-03-1943 | Aga Khan Palace Prison | The Government had blamed congress for disturbances. |
| 26. | 20 to 23-10-1946 | Delhi | For errors in a letter. |
| 27. | 15-08-1947 | Kolkata | Because of freedom and partition |
| 28. | 01 to 03-09-1947 | Kolkata | On own birthday |
| 29. | 13 to17-01-1948 | Delhi | Against communal riots. |

❑

# The Letters

Except the **'Complete Works of Mahatma Gandhi'** (CWMG), Pyarelal's and Tendulkar's Biographies of Gandhi, in all other books only the edited, shortened or parts of Gandhi's letters are printed. The missing matters are indicated by--------

So, when I was assigned the task to edit **'My Letters'** by Mahatma Gandhi, I decided to give complete letters as given in CWMG. (It is needless to state that all the letters have been taken from the original source 'CWMG.') I don't like to keep readers in doubt or dilemma. So, I have not used the dots that indicate something missing: words or sentences or paragraphs. These letters give a sense of completeness.

There was yet another reason behind giving complete letters. A particular editor has his choice and preference and may think some lines to be impertinent but for a reader those lines may be significant. The reader may feel them to be important. Different persons draw different conclusions, and explain and use them in different ways. As complete letters are given in **'My Letters'**, so the readers will have no complaints.

**'My Letters'** contains selected letters that Mahatma Gandhi wrote from time to time. He was a prolific writer. He answered all the letters that came to him, and wrote many on his own. This way, he wrote thousands of letters. It was not possible to collect all the letters, not even all the letters addressed to a single person. Here again, the readers must be reminded that the editors have their choice and preferences. The editor had the discretion in selecting letters and the recipients.

In **'My Letters'**, systematic efforts and a lot of trouble were taken to collect his letters written to selected persons. All the letters are significant, as they reveal the thought, views and programmes of Mahatma Gandhi. These are really important for general readers and the new generation which need an insight into the attitude and actions of Mahatma Gandhi and his insistent and incessant endeavour to get freedom for the country and to establish peace everywhere. The young and also not so-young will know Gandhi's opinion and efforts and also his rich and varied personality.

All the letters are important as they played a significant role in 'Indian Freedom Movement' and social life, and had an instant impact both on the rulers and the ruled. That is the reason his letters are important, and are being compiled and published at the time when instability and terror are at their respective peaks everywhere. These letters will show the desired effect once again.

Mahatma Gandhi wrote numerous letters to many different persons. He was very prompt in writing letters whenever he felt in need and in replying the letters. It is just a matter of conjecture how many of them were collected and how many of them were lost.

The letters of Gandhi reveal not only the subject and object well but also the person, personality and attitude of the writer. One can know real Gandhi through his letters.

Gandhi's determination and confidence, and his devotion and dedication towards the greater cause of nation and humanity have found profound expression in his letters.

Gandhi's letters are well reasoned out. They are a product of mind. There is hardly any space for emotions in them. But there is a really human aspect in his letters. It has not been shown or projected in the letters collected here. Yet it needs special mention, as it is vehemently there. Gandhi was not devoid of emotions. Some of his letters show emotions and emotional outbursts but on rare occasions and only in the letters that he wrote to console someone, when someone was seriously ill or at the demise of someone. Otherwise, his letters are free from emotions.

Gandhi's perception of each situation or issue was crystal clear and is shown well through his letters. There was no illusion or dilemma. He had no doubt about what he was doing or what he was telling the people. His ideas about almost everything were clear and clearly expressed in his letters. Such open and clear minds are rare. Without any shred of doubt, Gandhi was a rare figure.

The letters show that Gandhi had no ego. He was very humble and completely detached. He had no prejudice, not even against the person or persons who tried to inflict injuries on him. This is real non-violence. He was against inflicting mental injury to others, physical injury was not even in unknown dreams. There is no indication of ego or prejudice. Gandhi had only love and compassion; and the rest in him was for the people, ideals, own nation and other nations. His was a replica of divine nature. Naturally, he loved and belonged to humanity. He is an asset to every nation and the pride of many.

**'My Letters'** shows that Gandhi had a natural flair and command over writing letters. He has used no artificial ornamentation yet his letters are artistic and a proof of the refined sensibility and aesthetic sense of the writer. It is in-ornate yet beautiful, common, general and everyday prose, rhythmical in reading and easy to understand.

Gandhi wrote all types of letters: personal; objective, with or without purpose, for enquiry, for consoling, for chiding and guiding, for passing on information, official letters, public letters, political letters, business letters etc. in perfect professional style.

Gandhi wrote thousands of letters but never wasted his precious time and energy in unnecessarily expanding the length by totally excluding the extraneous matters. So, his letters are concise and compact. Naturally, they include from one line note to five printed pages but most of them are average in size, less than one printed page.

### Gandhi has signed his letters in many ways:

Bapu

Gandhi

M.K.Gandhi

Mohandas

Mohandas Gandhi

Gandhi's letters are passive and prosaic, mostly matter of fact, seldom emotional or poetic. Most of them reveal his programme and general worry.

□

SECTION-II

Selected But Complete Letters

# Letters to Motilal Nehru

Pandit Motilal Nehru was a rare dauntless and rigid figure; an intellectual of high order. He possessed sharp intelligence and immense courage. Patriotism was his strength and sacrifice his nature. He was a memorable figure and a power to reckon with in the struggle for India's independence. Many strange tales and unique anecdotes are famous about his life as a person, lawyer and freedom fighter.

Pandit Motilal Nehru was born in Agra on the 6th May, 1861. He had two brothers: Nandlal and Banshidhar. His father Pandit Gangadhar was Kotwal in Delhi. He studied for the first 12 years in different Maktabs then took admission in an English School in Kanpur. After passing the Matriculation Examination in Ist division, he took admission in Myore College, Allahabad. Later on, he passed the Law exam and started practice in Kanpur. He was one of the first four Advocates selected and appointed in Allahabad. He represented his clients wonderfully well, flourished as an advocate and became famous within no time. He bought a palace of a king which was named 'Anand Bhawan'. It became the centre of freedom fighters. Gandhi always stayed there whenever he was in Allahabad. Later on, Pandit Nehru dedicated this palace to the nation and it was rightly renamed as 'Swarajya Bhawan'.

Pandit Nehru joined Congress in 1888. He contributed in many ways in the publication of 'Leader' Newspaper. Later on, he started publishing his own newspaper, 'Independent.' Twice, he became the Congress President. He played a prominent role in the boycott of Simon Commission.

Motilal Nehru was a great fighter. He fought everywhere with all his might and mental acumen. During worst fight, he showed more vigour and intelligence for definite success.

Motilal Nehru and Mahatma Gandhi reciprocated well and respected one another.

ॐ

KUMARA PARK,
BANGALORE,
June 19, 1927

DEAR MOTILALJI,

I must still dictate, though this dictating is not to be regarded as any indication of weakness of body. I am simply literally following doctor's advice in order to store up energy for future use. Whether energy is being thereby stored or not remains to be known.

I have your telegram. If you could have braved the travelling through the hot parts, you would certainly have been amply rewarded and forgotten the heat of central India. I wonder whether chamber work could not be done outside Allahabad. Pherozshah used to drag clients after him. Of course it was cruel. I wonder whether for reasons of health you would not be justified in putting clients to the trouble of following you to a cool place.

Things, as they are shaping in the Congress, confirm the opinion that it is not yet time for Jawaharlal to shoulder the burden. He is too high-souled to stand the anarchy and hooliganism that seem to be growing in the Congress, and it would be cruel to expect him to evolve order all of a sudden out of chaos. I am confident, however, that the anarchy will spend itself before long and the hooligans will themselves want a disciplinarian.

Jawaharlal will come in then. For the present, we should press Dr. Ansari to take the reins. He won't control the hooligans. He will let them have their way; but he may specialise in the Hindu-Muslim question and do something in the matter. It will be quite enough work for him in the coming year to solve the almost insoluble problem.

Yours sincerely,

M. K. GANDHI

THE ASHRAM,
SABARMATI,
April 20, 1928

DEAR MOTILALJI,

I have your letter. I am daily making fresh discoveries which go to show that we may expect nothing from the mill-owners at the present stage. They will yield only to pressure and the pressure of the Government is more felt than that of the Congress. But we may not be impatient. We need not put boycott of Indian mill-made cloth in the same category as that of foreign cloth. A negative attitude about millcloth will be quite enough to keep the mills under wholesome check. A positive boycott will only stir up bad blood without bringing us any nearer boycott of foreign cloth. We shall never, unless a sudden manifestation of mass energy comes into being, succeed in reaching the millions. In spite of all we may do, for the time being the latter will therefore be buying Indian mill-cloth and, further, there will be keen competition between Lancashire mills and Japanese on the one hand and Indian mills on the other. We have therefore to concentrate our effort on changing the mentality of the townspeople and those few villagers whom we are controlling and bringing them round to the adoption of Khadi. If we set about doing this, the meassage of khadi will percolate the masses. Then both our and foreign mills will feel the brunt. That will be the time for our mills to come in a line with us. The moment they do so we can complete boycott of foreign cloth inside of six months. The programme definitely therefore has to be this :

We leave Indian mills severely alone. We carry on a whirlwind compaign for boycott of foreign cloth through khadi, asking people to count no sacrifice too great in adopting khadi. We must have faith in ourselves and in our people and believe that they can make this which appears to me to be small sacrifice. But I confess that at the present moment I do not visualise the organisation that is needed to carry on the boycott. The politicals who are in possession of the platform do not mean to do any serious business. They will not concentrate on any constructive work. Jawahar in a letter truly describes the atmosphere when he says: "There is violence in the air." We read and hear so much about the boycott of British cloth in Bengal, but the letters I receive almost every week show that there is no real boycott. There is no organisation behind it, there is no will working behind it. All things considered, what will you advise me to do?

The expected letter from Romain Rolland is due next Tuesday at the latest. I must after that come to a decision quickly. Supposing that Romain Rolland predisposes me in favour of the European visit, what would you have me to do in view of the talk of the boycott? Would you want me for the sake of the boycott not to go to Europe? I shall accept your decision whatever it may be. I am not personally keen on the European visit, but if all is plain sailing in India and if Romain Rolland wants me to visit Europe, I should feel bound to accept the European invitations. Will you please wire your decision? Jawahar will be with you and probably you will know Doctor Ansari's mind.

Yours sincerely,

M. K. GANDHI

DEAR MOTILALJI,

There has not been a moment to spare for writing work beyond what I have been able to snatch for Y.I. I have your wire today. I hope to reach Delhi on 17th instant via Marwar junction. The train reaches Delhi about 9.30 a.m. Rasik, my grandson, is lying on his deathbed in Delhi. He went there to teach carding to the Jamia boys. If he is still alive I shall drive straight to the Jamia and then attend the W.C. meeting. I do not know where I should stay this time. Usually I stay at Dr. Ansari's. May I look to you to decide and fix up wherever it is the most convenient. You will not detain me there longer than two days, I hope. 18th is a Monday. I would like to leave Delhi on 18th night.

I am under promise to finish Burma and Andhra before the end of April. I do not know how I shall cope with the two provinces now.

There has been a very good response to the Lalaji Memorial appeal in Sind.

Hope Kamala is better.

Yours sincerely,

M. K. GANDHI

[PS.]

*I reach Hyderabad on 13th and leave it 15th morning.*

ON THE TRAIN,
July 6, 1929

DEAR MOTILALJI,

I have slept over your proposal. But I feel I must not shoulder the burden. I am sure that Jawahar should preside. Let young men have their innings. We must stand behind them. There are a hundred reasons why I must not preside. There are five hundred to show why Jawahar should preside. If

39

you get this in time and if you approve I would deal with the matter in the next issue of *Young India*.

Yours,

M. K. GANDHI

❁ ❁ ❁

[On or after August 21, 1929]

DEAR MOTILALJI,

I have your second wire. I do not take the view you do about Jawahar. Jawaharlal would have been elected had I not been in the way. If the Congressmen concerned can be induced to think that I shall be of greater service without the chair they would surely have Jawahar. You may depend upon my not being unmindful of Jawahar's self-respect. I would not on any account thrust him on the country. But let us see how things shape. I shall take no hasty step.

I expect more news about Kamala. I hope she will now be entirely free from recurring pains and that this operation was all that was necessary to put her on her feet.

Yours,

M. K. GANDHI

❁ ❁ ❁

WARDHA,
December 14, 1929

DEAR MOTILALJI,

I wired you yesterday in answer to your letter that I shall be with you in Delhi on 22nd. I have since discovered that 23rd is a Monday. I do not know when the appointment with the Viceroy comes off. It must not be in the morning. If it is any time in the afternoon, there will be no difficulty. I would take silence on Sunday at about that hour. But what of our talk before the interview? My train reaches there at 11.28 a.m. If the interview takes place in the afternoon we would easily have some time on Sunday. The other way is for us to meet somewhere on the train and the third is for you to talk and for me, if I have anything to say, to put it down on paper. After all I have not much to say. At the interview you should lead. I do not know what I could say beyond reiterating the four conditions. As a matter of fact we go to listen to what H.E. has to say about our conditions. Now you will direct me.

I observe that your professional engagements keep you fully busy. I shall look forward to a fair share of the spoils. Daridranarayana's belly is never full.

Yours,

M. K. GANDHI

DELHI,
January 3, 1930

DEAR MOTILALJI,

In Lahore there was no time to talk or to read the newspaper or to think of anything else but the next hour's work. Here, in Delhi, on a cattle farm five miles away I saw the Hindustan Times and the Kelkar manifesto. It struck me immediately that it was absolutely necessary to have from you a brief statement to show why the boycott of Legislatures is an absolute necessity. The sooner you issue it to the Press, the better it would be. Jawahar surpassed all expectations. Even the critics were silenced. If we can but take some decisive step and come to grips this year it will be a fitting finish to the presidential year so well begun.

Yours,

SABARMATI,
January 20, 1930

DEAR MOTILALJI,

I have your letter. I did not realise you were so bad. In the circumstances there is no occasion for touring. After all we have said our say. Let those who wish seek election.

I do not think they will begin arrests so soon. But if they do, all the better. They are not likely to take all of us at the same time. If they do and if they put us all together, we shall have a rare time of it.

I am giving careful hints in Young India and Navajivan.

Yours sincerely,

M. K. GANDHI

[PS.]

*I am not writing to Jawaharlal today. The messenger is being detained for the time being.*

☐

# Letters to Jawahar Lal Nehru

Jawahar Lal Nehru participated in the freedom movement with all that he had: physical power, mental strength, material wealth and social status. He was a natural choice to become the first Prime Minister of India from the time of partition and freedom. He remained engrossed in the welfare of people and yet thought that he had not done all that he was capable of. So, he wrote on his pad the following lines of Robert Frost, the night before he died:

> The woods are lovely, dark and deep,
> And I have promises to keep,
> And miles to go before I sleep,
> And miles to go before I sleep.

Nehru was born in Allahabad on 14th November, 1889. His father Motilal Nehru was a famous lawyer and respected freedom fighter. His mother Shrimati Swarupa Rani Nehru was a respectable lady. He was taught at home by British and Irish teachers up to the age of fifteen. Next year, he was sent to England where he studied in a famous public school in Harrow and then at Oxford University. After becoming a barrister he returned back to India in 1912 and started his practice at Allahabad High Court.

Nehru met Gandhi for the first time in 1916 at Lucknow conference. He joined Congress and became the right hand man of Gandhi. In the same year, he was married to Kamla Rani of Delhi. The next year in 1917, Indira Priyadarshini was born to the couple.

Nehru remained the undisputed Prime Minister of India for 17 years; and kept the additional charge of Foreign Affairs in his hands. He was disillusioned after 1962 Chinese war and departed from the world on 27th May, 1964.

Gandhi and Nehru worked together for the freedom of the country but in philosophy, temperament and approach they were quite unlike one another.

Gandhi was the creative guiding force for all, while Nehru was the communicating link between several persons and different parties.

Gandhi was the confidence of the people of India and Nehru was the future hope for them.

Gandhi was adored, obeyed and followed, whereas Nehru was feared and loved also.

Gandhi diligently and Meticulously achieved greatness and became Mahatma, Bapu and Rashtrapita, the father of the biggest democracy of the world. Nehru was born with a silver spoon which he turned into golden. He inherited, saved and enlarged that inheritance.

ॐ

September 15, 1924

MY DEAR JAWAHARLAL,

I have your most touching personal letter. You will stand it all bravely I know. Father is just now in an irritable mood. And I am most anxious that neither you nor I should contribute an iota to the irritation. If it is at all possible you should have a frank chat with him and avoid such action as may offend him. It makes me unhappy to find him unhappy. His irritability is a sure sign of his unhappiness. Hasrat was here today and I find from him that even my proposal about spinning by every Congressman ruffles him. I do so feel like retiring from the Congress and doing the three things quietly. They are enough to occupy more than all the true men and women we can get. But even that ruffles people. I had a long chat with the Poona Swarajists. They will not agree to spin and they will not agree to my leaving the Congress. They do not realise that I shall cease to be useful as soon as I cease to be myself. It is a wretched situation but I do not despair. My faith is in God. I know only the moment's duty. It is given to me to know no more. Why then should I worry?

Shall I try to arrange for some money for you? Why may you not take up remunerative work? After all you must live by the sweat of your brow even though you may be under Father's roof. Will you be correspondent to some newspapers? Or will you take up a professorship?

Yours sincerely,

M.K. Gandhi

KUMARA PARK
Bangalore
July 20, 1927

MY DEAR JAWAHARLAL,

I have both your letters. Events have moved fairly fast between the dates of my letter and of the arrival of your letters. Sarojini Devi suggested under pressure from Muhamedbad and Mr. Jinha that I should press Father to accept the Presidential chair for the coming year. I totally dissented from her view and told her that Dr. Ansari was the only possible president though even he will be able to do precious little.

Things are going from bad to worse, and it is quite plain that we have not yet drunk the last dregs. But I regard all this rising of the poison to the surface as a neccessary process in national up-building. It is quite true that what was burrowing under the surface has now broken through the crust and allows itself to be seen by the naked eye.

I saw the other day in the daily press portraits of yourself, Kamala, Krishna and Indu, or was it you three without Indu, I now forget. You all seem to have grown fuller in the face and all over. I hope that the appearance coincides with the reality.

Though I am not yet physically quite strong, I have resumed the interrupted tour with considerable modifications and in gentle stages. I will not have resumed it but for the fact that collections were locked up and could not be freed unless I presented myself for receiving them.

Shankerlal and Anasuya Ben are just now eith me in addition to the party mentioned by me in my previous letter.

With Love,

BAPU

THE ASHRAM, SABARMATI,
January 17, 1928

MY DEAR JAWAHARLAL,

I must dictate and save time and give rest to my aching shoulder. I wrote to you on Sunday about Fenner Brockway. I hope you got that letter in due time.

Do you know that it was because you were the chief partner in the transactions referred to that I wrote the articles you have criticised, except of course about the so-called 'All-India Exhibition'? I felt a kind of safety that, in view of the relations between you and me, my writings would be taken in the spirit in which they were written. However, I see that they were a misfire all round. I do not mind it. For, it is evident that the articles alone could deliver you from the self-suppression under which you have been labouring apparently for so many years. Though I was beginning to detect some differences in viewpoint between you and me, I had no notion whatsoever of the terrible extent of these differences. Whilst you were heroically suppressing yourself for the sake of the nation and in the belief that by working with and under me in spite of yourself, you would serve the nation and come out scatheless, you were chafing under the burden of this unnatural self-suppression. And, while you were in that state, you overlooked the very things which appear to you now as my serious blemishes. I could show you from the pages of *Young India* equally strong articles written by me, when I was actively guiding the Congress with reference to the doings of the All-India Congress Committee. I have spoken similarly at the All-India Congress Committee meetings whenever there has been irresponsible and hasty talk or action. But whilst you were under stupefaction these things did not jar on you as they do now. And it seems to me, therefore, useless to show you the discrepancies in your letter. What I am now concerned with is future action.

If any freedom is required from me, I give you all the freedom you may need from the humble, unquestioning allegiance that you have given to me for all these years and which I value all the more for the knowledge I have now gained of your state. I see quite clearly that you must carry on open warfare against me and my views. For, if I am wrong I am evidently doing irreparable harm to the country and it is your duty after having known it to rise in revolt against me. Or, if you have any doubt as to the correctness of your conclusion, I shall gladly discuss them with you personally. The differences between you and me appear to me to be so vast and radical that there seems to be no meeting-ground between us. I can't conceal from you my grief that I should lose a comrade so valiant, so faithful, so able and so honest as you have always been; but in serving a cause, comradeships have got to be sacrificed. The cause must be held superior to all such considerations. But this dissolution of comradeship—if dissolution must come—in no way affects our personal intimacy. We have long become members of the same family, and we remain such in spite of grave political differences. I have the good fortune to enjoy such relations with several people. To take Sastri for instance, he and I differ in the political outlook as poles asunder, but the bond between him and me that sprung up before we knew the political differences has persisted and survived the fiery ordeals it had to go through.

I suggest a dignified way of unfurling your banner. Write to me a letter for publication showing your differences. I will print it in *Young India* and write a brief reply. Your first letter I destroyed after reading and replying to it, the second I am keeping, and if you do not want to take the trouble of writing another letter, I am prepared to publish the letter that is before me. I am not aware of any offensive passage in it. But if I find any, you may depend upon my removing every such passage. I consider that letter to be a frank and honest document.

With love,

BAPU

SATYAGRAHA ASHRAM,
SABARMATI,
February 26, 1928

MY DEAR JAWAHAR,

I have your letters. I am sensing all that is going on in Delhi and can understand every word of what you have said in your letter. I can't give you an adequate conception of my grief as I follow the Conference proceedings from day to day and read between the lines. Father's illuminating letter only confirmed my own reading from a distance. Then came Kripalani's letter yesterday to Krishnadas, and yours has come today to put the finishing touch. What a miserable show we are putting up against the insolence of Lord Birkenhead and the crookedness of the Commissioners? I had not expected much from Sir John Simon, but I was not at all prepared for his resorting to all the known tricks of bureaucracy, and this the latest trade on untouchables adds to the ugliness of the whole picture. However, we have to be patient. You must therefore patiently go through the agony and mend where you can.

Do come as early as possible. I hope Kamala is keeping up her strength, if not actually adding to it. I wonder if Father has told you that, before you came, when Father was with me in Bangalore, he and I had contemplated your stay in Bangalore because of its magnificent climate during summer. There are just four weeks of somewhat trying weather, but you could always go to Nandi Hill only 35 miles from Bangalore where you have delightfully cool weather. In no case should Kamala be allowed to lose what she gained in Switzerland.

Yours sincerely,

BAPU

SATYAGRAHASHRAM,
SABARMATI,
March 20, 1928

MY DEAR JAWAHAR,

I have received your two letters. I write just now only to fulfil the promise to send you a message for the friend you mentioned. He has now written directly to me, but as I promised the message to you, here it is.

I hope you are following my articles on boycott and mills. I am having conferences with the mill-owners also. Whether they will come to anything I do not know. But if anything appears to you wrong or weak you will please let me know.

How is Kamala doing? Where are you going to keep her during the hot season?

Yours sincerely,

BAPU

MY DEAR JAWAHAR,

I have your letter. The enclosed copies will tell you what progress is being made in the negotiations with the mill-owners. I however agree with you that nothing will come out of them at the present moment. But the negotiations may fructify on due occasion. There was a time when the mill-owners were absolutely defiant about boycott propaganda. I shall write to you after these negotiations are finished.

Though Romain Rolland's first expected letter has arrived and [he] warmly looks [forward] to my proposed visit, it does not enable me to come to a decision. As the time for arriving at a fixed decision is drawing nearer, my diffidence is growing. There may be however a cable from Rolland next week and it may decide my fate.

Meanwhile there is no going to Singapur. I am fixed up here for the time being. If I do not go to Europe, I am due to go to Burma and pass there two months, going to a hill-side and making collections during my stay there.

I am quite of your opinion that some day we shall have to start an intensive movement without the rich people and witout the vocal educated class. But that time is not yet.

You do not tell me where Kamala is to pass the summer months.

Yours sincerely,

BAPU

THE ASHRAM,
SABARMATI,
April 5, 1928

MY DEAR JAWAHAR,

You will see my article on mills in the current issue of *"Young India"*. The latest move is on their own to start a

Swadeshi League without reference to us. Do not think anything concrete is going to come out of my effort. By all means let them prosecute their own plans. So far as I can see, we must confine our attention to Khadi hawking.

No final decision has yet been arrived at about the European visit. I am shirking it and making it depend upon some further indication from Rolland which I should have next week.

Yours sincerely,

BAPU

THE ASHRAM,
SABARMATI,
April 17, 1928

MY DEAR JAWAHAR,

I have your letter. Do you know that even when you wrote to me that you were going to the Punjab, I did not know that you were going as the president of the Conference? When Dr. Kitchlew wrote to me, he said nothing about who the president was to be. However I was glad when I learnt that you presided.

Of course I notice everywhere what you noticed at the Conference. I wonder if you have noticed what I sense everywhere, utter absence of seriousness and disinclination to do any concrete work demanding sustained energy.

Do you find any hope in the Punjab for Hindu-Muslim unity?

About the European visit, I can give you no definite news yet.

The fiasco about mills you know everything by this time from Father.

With Love,

BAPU

MY DEAR JAWAHAR,

I have your letter. Of course you know already the calamity that has befallen me on the death of Maganlal. It is well-nigh unbearable. However I am putting a brave front.

I had not read the resolution asking the Congress to drop "peaceful and legitimate means" and change the expression into "by all possible means". Independence I can swallow, "by all means" is unswallowable. But I suppose we shall have to develop a stomach strong enough to swallow any poison. I hope however that you will not allow yourself to be exploited beyond your wish and capacity.

The mill-owners, it has now become obviously clear, wanted to do a deal with the Congress. But I am not sorry for these abortive negotiations. They have cleared the atmosphere.

The expected letter from Romain Rolland was received on Sunday. He will not bear the burden I wanted him to do. So I am not going this year. But you will read about this in the pages of *"Young India"*.

Yours sincerely,

BAPU

SATYAGRAHASHRAM,
SABARMATI,
November 17, 1928

DEAR FRIEND,

I have your letters. I would like you first of all to tell me what you want to confer with me about. I cannot possibly trouble you to come to Sabarmati or to Wardha where I expect to proceed shortly.

With reference to your intention to stay at the Ashram for some days, I am sorry that it will not be possible. The

Ashram or rather the Udyoga Mandir is under the control of a board of management.

Yours sincerely,

BAPU

SATYAGRAHASHRAM,
SABARMATI,
November 17, 1928

MY DEAR JAWAHAR,

Your letter frees me from all anxiety. So long as you are willing to act as Agent, no change need be made, and certainly not whilst there is rumour of your being spirited away. When that event happens, we shall see. Personally I like the idea of Kripalani becoming Agent when you can no longer shoulder the burden. We shall discuss the matter further if you can come to Wardha on the 18th December or we shall do so in Calcutta.

Sitla Sahai wanted to be in the Ashram for some months for mental adjustment more than anything else. He has domestic and other worries preying upon him. He wanted a quiet time and he is having it. I am sorry about Kamala. Evidently she never completely recovered in Switzerland. I am glad you are taking her to Calcutta. She will at least have the best advice possible. I hope you are not overworking yourself. Lalaji's death is a great calamity.

Yours sincerely,

BAPU

PARNAKUTI
POONA,
September 14, 1933

MY. DEAR JAWAHARLAL,

I am glad you have written so fully and frankly.

When, on my return from London at the end of 1931, I found you to have been suddenly snatched away from me, I felt the separation keenly. I was, therefore, most anxious to meet you and exchange views.

With much of what you have said in your letter I am in complete agreement. The experience gained after the Karachi Congress has, if possible, strengthened my faith in the main resolution and the economic programme referred to by you. I have no doubt in my mind that our goal can be no less than 'Complete Independence'. I am also in whole-hearted agreement with you when you say that without a material revision of vested interests the condition of the masses can never be improved. I believe, too, though I may not go as far as you do, that before India can become one homogeneous entity, the princes will have to part with much of their power and become popular representatives of the people over whom they are ruling today. I can corroborate from first-hand experience much of what you say about the Round Table Conference. Nor have I the slightest difficulty in agreeing with you that in these days of rapid intercommunication and a growing consciousness of the oneness of all mankind, we must recognise that our nationalism must not be inconsistent with progressive internationalism. India cannot stand in isolation and unaffected by what is going on in other parts of the world. I can, therefore, go the whole length with you and say that 'we should range ourselves with the progressive forces of the world'. But I know that though there is such an agreement between you and me in the enunciation of ideals, there are temperamental differences between us. Thus you have emphasised the necessity of a clear statement of the goal, but having once determined it, I have never attached importance to the repetition. The clearest possible definition of the goal and its appreciation would fail to take us there if we do not know and utilise the means of achieving it. I have, therefore, concerned myself principally with the conservation of the means and their progressive use. I know

54

that if we can take care of them, attainment of the goal is assured. I feel too that our progress towards the goal will be in exact proportion to the purity of our means. If we can give an ocular demonstration of our uttermost truthfulness and non-violence, I am convinced that our statement of the national goal cannot long offend the interests which your letter would appear to attack. We know that the princes, the zamindars, and those who depend for their existence upon the exploitation of the masses, would cease to fear and distrust us, if we could but ensure the innocence of our methods. We do not seek to coerce any. We seek to convert them. This method may appear to be long, perhaps too long, but I am convinced that it is the shortest.

In the main I agree with your interpretation of Sjt. Aney's instructions and my note upon them. I am quite clear in my mind that had those instructions not been issued, the whole movement of civil resistance would have collapsed through growing internal weakness; for Congressmen were deluding themselves into the belief that there were organisations effectively functioning to which they could look for guidance, when, as a matter of fact, under the organised terrorism which the Ordinance Rule means, organised functioning of Congress Committees had become impossible. A false belief in the functioning of organisations, rendered illegal and largely impotent, was fast producing a demoralisation which had to be arrested. There is no such thing as demoralization in civil resistance properly applied. You have said rightly that after all "civil disobedience is essentially an individual affair". I go a step further and say that so long as there is one civil resister offering resistance, the movement cannot die and must succeed in the end. Individual civil resisters do not need the aid of an organisation. After all an organisation is nothing without the individuals composing it. Sjt. Aney's instructions were, therefore, I hold, an affective answer to the Ordinances and if only men and women belonging to the Congress will appreciate the necessity of those instructions with all their implications, the Ordinances will be rendered nugatory, at least so far as the resisters are concerned. They can form a nucleus around which an army of invincible civil resisters can be built up. Nothing in Sjt. Aney's instructions or in my note would warrant the supposition that they preclude organised action by Congressmen in any shape or form.

I would like to warn you against thinking that there is no fundamental difference between individual civil resistance and mass civil resistance. I think that the fundamental difference is implied in your own admission that "it is essentially an individual affair". The chief distinction between mass civil resistance and individual civil resistance is that in the latter everyone is a complete independent unit and his fall does not affect the others; in mass civil resistance the fall of one generally adversely affects the rest. Again, in mass civil resistance leadership is essential, in individual civil resistance every resister is his own leader. Then again, in mass civil resistance, there is a possibility of failure; in individual civil resistance failure is an impossibility. Finally, a State may cope with mass civil resistance; no State has yet been found able to cope with individual civil resistance.

Nor may much be made of my statement that an organisation which feels its own strength can at its own risk adopt mass civil resistance. While, as an opinion, it is unexceptionable, I know that at the present moment there is no organisation that can shoulder the burden. I do not want to raise false hopes.

Now about the secret methods. I am as firm as ever that they must be tabooed. I am myself unable to make any exceptions. Secrecy has caused much mischief and if it is not put down with a firm hand, it may ruin the movement. There may be exceptional circumstances that may warrant secret methods. I would forgo that advantage for the sake of the masses whom we want to educate in fearlessness. I will not confuse their minds by leading them to think that under certain circumstances, they may resort to secret methods. Secrecy is inimical to the growth of the spirit of civil resistance. If Congressmen will realise that all property is liable to be confiscated at any moment, they will learn to be utterly independent of it.

I quite agree with you that it is ludicrous for individuals to send notices to the local authorities of their intention to offer a particular form of civil disobedience. We do not want to make a great movement ridiculous. Therefore when civil resistance is offered it should be offered seriously and in an effective manner, in so far as this is possible, in furtherance of the Congress programme.

I notice one gap in your letter. You make no mention of the various constructive activities of the Congress. They became an integral part of the Congress programme that was framed after mature deliberations in 1920. With civil resistance as the background we cannot possibly do without the constructive activities such as communal unity, removal of untouchability and universalisation of the spinning-wheel and khaddar. I am as strong as ever about these. We must recognise that whilst the Congressmen can be counted by hundreds of thousands, civil resisters imprisoned have never amounted to more than one lakh at the outside. I feel that there is something radically wrong if paralysis has overtaken the remaining lakhs. There is nothing to be ashamed of in an open confession by those who for any reason whatsoever are unable to join the civil resisters' ranks. They are also serving the cause of the country and bringing it nearer to the goal who are engaged in any of the constructive activities I have named and several other kindred activities I can add to the list. Ordinance or no Ordinance, if individual Congressmen and Congresswomen will learn the art of contributing their share to the work of building of the house of independence and realise their own importance, dark as the horizon seems to us, there is absolutely no cause for despair or disappointment.

Finally, if I can say so without incurring the risk of your accusing me of egotism, I would like to say that I have no sense of defeat in me and the hope in me that this country of ours is fast marching towards its goal is burning as bright as it did in 1920; for I have an undying faith in the efficacy of civil resistance. But as you are aware, after full and prayerful consideration, I have decided not to take the offensive during the unexpired period of the sentence of imprisonment that was pronounced against me on the 4th of August last by the court that met in Yeravda Jail. I need not go into the reasons as I have already issued a separate statement about it. This personal suspension, although it may be misunderstood for a while, will show how and when it may become a duty. And if it is a duty, it cannot possibly injure the cause.

Yours,

BAPU

JAWAHARLAL NEHRU
POONA

Novermber 1, 1933

MY DEAR JAWAHARLAL,

Your several letters to hand. I see you have handed to the Press the two resignations. They should clear the air a bit. I do not follow the Hindu Sabha activities. They are vicious. It is most unscrupulous if they are making use of my name in connection with shuddhi. If you have any literature please pass it on to me. I think that the nationalist Press so called or real has not welcomed its activities and has been known often to condemn it. I do not know anything about the embargo on M. A. K. Azad's book. As to the Harijan activities, the complaint is wholly unjustified. My conscience is absolutely clear. So far as you and I are concerned, we can clear our minds and hands by exchanging letters, if you like. I do not know what aggressive action is possible or desirable beyond an emphatic condemnation of specific acts.

As to Gorakhpur, I do not see what can be done. I am finding it hard to get funds for your workers and the Dal people. I am still talking about both. Baba Raghavdas told me he was trying grain collections for the peasants in distress. He is under promise to send me authentic details of persecution.

Nariman was here yesterday. I have advised him to see you and told him that you were my political chief! What else could I do ? I stand thoroughly discredited as a religious maniac and predominantly a social worker. I told him that if I felt convinced that the A.I.C.C. members desired discontinuance of C. D. and a council-entry programme, I would at once ask you to convene a meeting of A.I.C.C. I do not do so because I believe that the majority will insist on a C. D. programme and I do not want to invite the ordinance sword for it. I have told him too that I would not resist any programme that the A.I.C.C. might want though I could not give my approval to the suspension of C. D. I believe Kelkar's attitude to be honest and consistent. He frankly dislikes N. C. O. and C. D. He would not join the terrorists or whatever they may be called. Then for a man of political activity, council-entry is the only programme such as it is. Hopeless inactivity is the worst of all and should be discountenanced.

I think I have now covered all the points raised in your letters and even not raised. It is nearing 4 a. m.

Hope Mother's progress continuing. Herewith note for Kamala.

Love.

BAPU

August 14, 1934

MY DEAR JAWAHARLAL,

Though you are now under distressing circumstances, your release takes a great load off my mind, as it is three-fourths medicine for Kamala. I have missed you greatly during all the momentous steps I have taken. But of these when we meet.

I am well, though the last day proved the most trying of all the days and washed me out thoroughly. But I have no doubt that I shall pick up quickly.

This is however to suggest to you that you should not make any public political pronouncement. I have felt that in cases of domestic illness or sorrow the Government has acted in a becoming manner. I do feel therefore that we ought to recognise this fact by not using the liberty thus obtained for any other purpose not inconsistent with that of the Government. I feel that this is due to them and to ourselves, especially when civil resistance is suspended. If my argument appeals to your reason, you will announce your self-restraint in a fitting manner. When Kamala is better I expect you to come here.

BAPU

August 17, 1934

MY DEAR JAWAHARLAL,

Your passionate and touching letter deserves a much longer reply than my strength will permit.

I had expected fuller grace from the Government. However your presence has done for Kamala and incidentally for Mama what no drugs or doctors could have done. I hope that you will be allowed to remain longer than the very few days you expect.

I understand your deep sorrow. You are quite right in giving full and free expression to your feelings. But I am quite sure that from our common standpoint a closer study of the written word will show you that there is not enough reason for all the grief and disappointment you have felt. Let me assure you that you have not lost a comrade in me. I am the same as you knew me in 1917 and after. I have the same passion that you knew me to possess for the common goal. I want complete independence for the country in the full English sense of the term. And every resolution that has pained you had been framed with that end in view. I must take full responsibility for the resolutions and the whole conception surrounding them.

But I fancy that I have the knack for knowing the need of the time. And the resolutions are a response thereto. Of course here comes in the difference of our emphasis on the method or the means which to me are just as important as the goal and in a sense more important in that we have some control over them whereas we have none over the goal if we lose control over the means.

Do read the resolution about 'loose talk' dispassionately. There is not a word in it about socialism. Greatest consideration has been paid to the socialists some of whom I know so intimately. Do I not know their sacrifice? But I have found them as a body to be in a hurry. Why should they not be? Only, if I cannot march quite as quick, I must ask them to halt and take me along with them. That is literally my attitude. I have looked up the dictionary meaning of socialism. It takes me no further than where I was before I read the definition. What will you have me to read to know its full content? I have read one of the books Masani gave me and now I am devoting all my spare time to reading the book recommended by Narendra Deva.

You are hard on the members of the Working Committee. They are our colleagues such as they are. After all we are a free institution. They must be displaced, if they do not deserve confidence. But it is wrong to blame them for their inability to undergo the sufferings that some others have gone through.

After the explosion I want construction. Therefore now, lest we do not meet, tell me exactly what you will have me to do and who you think will best represent your views.

As to the trust, I was not present. Vallabhbhai was. Your attitude betrays anger. You should trust the trustees to do their duty. I did not think there was anything wrong. I was too preoccupied to concentrate on it. I shall now study the papers and everything. Of course your feelings will be fully respected by other trustees. Having given you this assurance, I would ask you not to take this matter so personally as you have done. It more becomes your generous nature to give the same credit to your co-trustees for regard for Father's memory that you would take for yourself. Let the nation be the custodian of Father's memory and you only as one of the nation.

I hope Indu is well and likes her new life. And what about Krishna?

Love.

BAPU

WARDHA,
September 12, 1935

MY DEAR JAWAHARLAL,

How well you have joined Kamala! It is the best tonic for her. I shall keep a note for her herewith. Your messages are being duly received here. And Sarup repeats what she receives. Let us hope all will end well. Please thank Dr. Atal for his messages and letters which have been most helpful. I expect a regular mail from you whilst the crisis lasts. Typed sheets are with me. I shall go through them as soon as possible.

Mahadev had to go to Bombay to help Vallabhbhai about an inquiry. And he is still there. Rajagopalachari has just dropped in with Laxmi and her baby boy. Devdas was badly ill. Ansari has packed him off to Simla. I have Mira on my hands prostrate with bad fever.

I would like you to allow yourself to be elected President for the next year. Your acceptance will solve many difficulties. If you think fit, send me a wire.

Has Indu been fixed up?

Khurshed is here. She will be writing to you by the ordinary mail.

Love from us all.

BAPU

May 29, 1936

MY DEAR JAWAHARLAL,

I have your letter of 25th instant. So you are touring with almost feverish speed. May you have the requisite strength. Even a week at Khali will be a godsend.

I propose to make public use of your statement on khadi. I have received so many inquiries. The distorted summary has caused consternation among our people who have faith in khadi. Your statement will ease the situation a bit.

Your explanation about the omission of a woman on the W. C. does not give me satisfaction. If you had shown the slightest desire to have a woman on the Committee, there would have been no difficulty whatsoever about any of the older ones standing out. There was pressure if it may be so called only about Bhulabhai. And the first time his name was mentioned you had no objection. There was no pressure about any other member. And then you had this unfettered choice of omitting a socialist name and taking a

63

woman. But so far as I remember you yourself had difficulty in choosing a substitute for Sarojini Devi and you were anxious to omit her. You even went so far as to say that you did not believe in the tradition or convention of always having a woman and a certain number of Mussalmans on the cabinet. Therefore so far as the exclusion of [a] woman is concerned, I think it was your own unfettered discretion. No other member would have had the desire or the courage to break the convention. I must also tell you that in certain Congress circles the whole blame is being thrown on me, for I am reported to have excluded Mrs. Naidu and to have insisted on having no woman–a thing for which as I said to you I had not even the courage. I could not exclude even Mrs. N., not to mention a woman.

As to the other members too, I have been under the impression that you chose the members because it was the right thing to do for the cause. There was no question of *behaya* or *hayadar* when all were actuated by the noblest of motives, i.e., service of the cause according to their lights. I may say that your statement which your letter confirms has given much pain to Rajen Babu, C. R. and Vallabhbhai. They feel –and I agree with them–they have tried to act honourably and with perfect loyalty towards you as a colleague. Your statement makes you out to be the injured party. I wish you could see this viewpoint and correct the report if it is at all possible.

As to the third thing. I would love to have the thing cleared. I cannot guess what you want to say. But that must wait till we meet. I must not add to the strain you are already bearing.

About Dr. Ansari Memorial, I have given Asaf Ali my clear opinion that the memorial for the Doctor should await better times politically as it has for Papa. Do you think otherwise?

The Kamala memorial is making slow progress.

Herewith the Princess's letter containing a reference to Indu.

Love.

BAPU

[PS.]

*Bangalore City till 10th.*

SEGAON, WARDHA,
July 15, 1937

MY DEAR JAWAHARLAL,

Today is the election day. I am watching.

But this I write to tell you that I have begun to write on the function of Congress Ministries and allied topics. I hesitated but I saw that it was my duty to write, when I felt so keenly. I wish I could send you an advance copy of my article for *Harijan*. Mahadev will see this. If he has a copy he will send it. When you see it, you will please tell me if I may continue to write so. I do not want to interfere with your handling of the whole situation. For, I want the maximum from you for the country. I would be doing distinct harm, if my writing disturbed you.

I hope you got my letter about the Maulana.

Love.

BAPU

ON THE TRAIN,
August 4, 1937

MY DEAR JAWAHARLAL,

I am stupid. On receiving your letter I searched my file and behold! I found the cutting containing Meherally's speech. I referred to his, not Masani's speech.

This is being written in a terribly jolting train taking me back to Wardha. It is now 10.30 p.m. I woke up from sleep, thought of the speech and began the search. Yesterday's compartment was better.

I saw the Viceroy. You will have seen the communique. It correctly summarises the interview. There were other incidental things which Kripalani will mention to you when he meets you. One thing I may mention here. He might invite you as he invited me. I told him that if the invitation was sent, you were not likely to refuse it. Was I right?

I am sorry for having inflicted Roy's speeches on you. But I think you were bound to read them. However I am in no hurry to have your opinion on them. You may take your time unless you have already read them.

I note that you are having the operation for Indu in Bombay.

Love.

BAPU

ON THE TRAIN TO PESHAWAR,
April 30, 1938

MY DEAR JAWAHARLAL,

Here is a copy of the brief notes I have jotted down of the $3^1/_2$ hours' talks with Jinnah. It may be that you and the other members may not like the basis. Personally I see no escape from it. My handicap today is that I do not move about the country, as you do, and a still more serious handicap is the inner despondency that has overtaken me. I am carrying on, but it is galling to me to think that I have lost the self-confidence that I possessed only a month ago. I hope that this is but a temporary phase in my life. I have mentioned this to help you to examine the proposals on their merits. I do not suppose the first will present any difficulty. The second is novel, with all its implications. You will not hesitate summarily to reject it if it does not commend itself to you. In this matter you will have to give the lead.

I expect to return on the 11th. Subhas in reply to my telegram suggesting that he should open formal negotiations with Jinnah telegraphs that he will be in Bombay on the 10th. I wish that you could also go there early. I am writing to Maulana Saheb in the same strain sending him a copy of this letter.

Love.

BAPU

SEVAGRAM, WARDHA,
February 3, 1939

MY DEAR JAWAHARLAL,

After the election and the manner in which it was fought, I feel that I shall serve the country by absenting myself from the Congress at the forthcoming session. Moreover, my health is none too good. I would like you to help me. Please do not press me to attend.

I hope the rest at Khali has done you and Indu good. Indu ought to write to me.

Love.

BAPU

WARDHA,
October 24, 1940

DEAR JAWAHARLAL,

I was glad to have your wire. If my statement has been allowed, you will have seen it before this.

If you are ready, you may now ceremonially declare your civil disobedience. I would suggest your choosing a village for your audience. I do not suppose they will allow you to repeat your speech. They were not ready with their plans so far as Vinoba was concerned. But should they let you free

I suggest your following the plan laid down for Vinoba. But if you feel otherwise, you will follow your own course. Only I would like you to give me your programme. You will fix your own date so as to leave me time for announcing the date and place. It may be that they won't let you even fulfil your very first programme. I am prepared for every such step on the part of the Government. Whilst I would make use of every legitimate method seeking publicity for our programme, my reliance is on regulated thought producing its own effect. If this is hard for you to believe, I would ask you to suspend judgment and watch results. I know you will yourself be patient and ask our people on your side to do likewise. I know what strain you are bearing in giving me your loyalty. I prize it beyond measure. I hope it will be found to have been well-placed, for it is 'do or die'. There is no turning back. Our case is invulnerable. There is no giving in. Only I must be allowed to go my way in demonstrating the power of non-violence when it is unadulterated.

Maulana Saheb telephoned saying I should choose another man for the second satyagraha. I told him I could not do so if you consented to come in.

I would like your reaction to the step I have taken regarding *Harijan*.

Love.

BAPU

SEVAGRAM, WARDHA,
April 15, 1942

CHI. JAWAHARLAL,

The Professor is here. He has told me everything. I also heard about your Press interview. Whereas we have always had differences of opinion it appears to me that now we also differ in practice. What can Vallabhbhai and others do in such a situation? If your policy is accepted the Committee should not retain its present shape.

The more I think of it the more I feel that you are making a mistake. I see no good in American troops entering India and in our resorting to guerrilla warfare.

It is my duty to caution you.

I hope Indu and Feroze are well.

Blessings from

BAPU

[PS.]

*I heard yesterday that the Forward Bloc people in Utkal are armed and that the Communists are ready for guerrilla warfare. I do not know how much truth there is in it.*

SEVAGRAM, WARDHA,
July 13, 1942

CHI. JAWAHARLAL,

I have read the resolution. I note that you have tried to include some of my points. I do not desire any modification.

But I do desire that, as far as possible, all of us should interpret the appeal in the same way. It will not be good if we speak in different voices.

I stick to the hundred per cent support I gave you in what you said about yourself. I have thought over the matter a great deal and still feel that your capacity for service will increase if you withdraw. And to that extent you will find satisfaction. You may attend the Committee occasionally as I do or as Narendra Dev does. This will ensure your help being available and at the same time your fully retaining your freedom.

This is my plea about Maulana Saheb. I find that the two of us have drifted apart. I do not understand him nor does he understand me. We are drifting apart on the Hindu-Muslim question as well as on other questions. I have also a suspicion that Maulana Saheb does not entirely approve of the proposed action. No one is at fault. We have to face the facts. Therefore I suggest that the Maulana should relinquish Presidentship but remain in the Committee, the Committee should elect an interim President and all should proceed unitedly. This great struggle cannot be conducted properly without unity and without a President who comes forth with a hundred per cent co-operation.

Please show this letter to Maulana Saheb. At the moment it is intended for you two only. If you do not like either or both of my suggestions, you may reject them. My motive in writing this is only to help. Whether you approve of it or not, it should not cause any unpleasantness.

The date and venue for the A.I.C.C. have not been indicated in your draft.

As far as I am concerned, you are free to issue this appeal to the Press.

It is not necessary to come here for a discussion of the resolution. But it has to be as Maulana Saheb orders.

Blessings from

BAPU

October 5, 1945

CHI. JAWAHARLAL,

I have long been intending to write to you but can do so only today. I have also been wondering whether I should write in English or Hindustani. In the end I have decided to write in Hindustani.

I take first the sharp difference of opinion that has arisen between us. If such a difference really exists people should also know about it, for the work of swaraj will suffer if they are kept in the dark. I have said that I fully stand by the kind of governance which I have described in *Hind Swaraj*. It is not just a way of speaking. My experience has confirmed the truth of what I wrote in 1909. If I were the only one left who believed in it, I would not be sorry. For I can only testify to the truth as I see it. I have not *Hind Swaraj* in front of me. It is better that I redraw the picture today in my own language. Then it would not matter to me whether or no the picture tallies with that of 1909, nor should it to you. I do not have to establish what I had said before. What is worth knowing is only what I have to say today. I believe that if India, and through India the world, is to achieve real freedom, then sooner or later we shall have to go and live in the villages— in huts, not in palaces. Millions of people can never live in cities and palaces in comfort and peace. Nor can they do so by killing one another, that is, by resorting to violence and untruth. I have not the slightest doubt that, but for the pair, truth and non-violence, mankind will be doomed. We can have the vision of that truth and non-violence only in the simplicity of the villages. That simplicity resides in the spinning-wheel and what is implied by the spinningwheel. It does not frighten me at all that the world seems to be going in the opposite direction. For the matter of that, when the moth approaches its doom it whirls round faster and faster till it is burnt up. It is possible that India will not be able to escape this moth-like circling. It is my duty to try, till my last breath, to save India and through it the world from such a fate. The sum and substance of what I want to say is that the individual person should have control over the things that are necessary for the sustenance of life. If he cannot have such control the individual cannot survive. Ultimately, the world is made up only of individuals. If there were no drops there would be no ocean. This is only a rough and ready statement. There is nothing new in this.

But even in *Hind Swaraj* I have not said all this. While I appreciate modern thought, I find that an ancient thing, considered in the light of this thought looks so sweet. You will not be able to understand me if you think that I am talking about the villages of today. My ideal village still exists only in my imagination. After all every human

71

being lives in the world of his own imagination. In this village of my dreams the villager will not be dull—he will be all awareness. He will not live like an animal in filth and darkness. Men and women will live in freedom, prepared to face the whole world. There will be no plague, no cholera and no smallpox. Nobody will be allowed to be idle or to wallow in luxury. Everyone will have to do body labour. Granting all this, I can still envisage a number of things that will have to be organised on a large scale. Perhaps there will even be railways and also post and telegraph offices. I do not know what things there will be or will not be. Nor am I bothered about it. If I can make sure of the essential thing, other things will follow in due course. But if I give up the essential thing, I give up everything.

The other day, at the final day's meeting of the Working Committee, we had taken a decision to the effect that the Working Committee would meet for two or three days to work out this very thing. I shall be happy if it meets. But even if it does not meet, I want that we two should understand each other fully. And this for two reasons. Our bond is not merely political. It is much deeper. I have no measure to fathom that depth. This bond can never be broken. I therefore want that we should understand each other thoroughly in politics as well. The second reason is that neither of us considers himself as worthless. We both live only for India's freedom, and will be happy to die too for that freedom. We do not care for praise from any quarter. Praise or abuse are the same to us. They have no place in the mission of service. Though I aspire to live up to 125 years rendering service, I am nevertheless an old man, while you are comparatively young. That is why I have said that you are my heir. It is only proper that I should at least understand my heir and my heir in turn should understand me. I shall then be at peace.

One thing more. I had written to you about Kasturba Trust and Hindustani. You had said you would write after thinking things over. I find that your name is already figuring in the Hindustani Sabha. Nanavati reminded me that he had approached you and Maulana Saheb and that you had appended your signature. That was in 1942. That was long ago. You know where Hindustani stands today. If you still stand by that signature, I wish to get some work out of you in this regard. It will not involve much running about, but some work will be called for.

The work of Kasturba Memorial Trust is rather complicated. I realise that if what I have said above is going to irk you or is irking you, you will not feel comfortable even in the Kasturba Trust.

The last point concerns the sparks that are flying about in the conflict with Sarat Babu. I have been pained by the episode. I have been unable to trace it to its root. If what you have told me is all there is to it and nothing more remains to be said, then I do not have to inquire further. But if an explanation seems necessary, I very much want to hear it.

If we have to meet to thrash out all these matters, then we should find time for a meeting.

You are working very hard. I trust you are in good health and Indu is well.

Blessings from

BAPU

PANCHGANI,
July 17, 1946

MY DEAR JAWAHARLAL,

I have gone through what Munshi showed me, though I did not have the time to examine it closely. He came today after 4 o'clock and will be going back tomorrow morning. I had a long talk with him about grouping. He will explain things to you. I have advised him to consult other lawyers as well. What he has prepared after seven days' labours may not be placed before the Committee just yet. Once it goes before the Committee, it will become public. I do not see the need of making it public so soon.

Your statement as published in the papers does not sound good. If it is correctly reported, some explanation is needed. It must be admitted that we have to work within the limits of the State Paper. It is clear in Maulana's letters. We have given it our own inter-pretation. But if the Federal Court gives a different interpretation, we shall have to be firm. I think it necessary to say this clearly. If we do not admit even this much, we will be doing nothing and Jinnah Saheb's accusation will prove true.

Fischer and Jayaprakash have come here today. They too will return tomorrow.

Blessings from

BAPU

[PS.]

*In regard to Kashmir, Sardar has sent me the Maharaja's speech. It deserves careful study. I think a meeting of the Working Committee should be called to consider it. Let us not be hasty. Let us not endanger the whole thing just for this reason. I am of the view that Maulana Saheb and, if necessary, Sardar too, should go to Kashmir. After all, has not the Working Committee assumed the entire responsibility?*

BAPU

HARIJAN COLONY,
NEW DELHI,
August 29, 1946

CHI. JAWAHARLAL,

We never have a moment to ourselves. I do not ask for it. You never have any time to spare. Nor do I have any. So a good many matters remain untouched.

I have before me your letter of the 20th. It came to me yesterday *via* Wardha. It dwells on the question of who

74

should be the Congress President in view of the fact that you will be the Prime Minister. You incline in favour of Maulana Saheb. This I do not understand and cannot understand. In my view, Maulana Saheb should not accept nomination. Maulana Saheb hesitates to accept ministership. The responsibilities of the President, especially in the present juncture, are I feel arduous. But in my view it is not the only reason why he should not be president. I cannot accept, too, that other than Maulana Saheb, Sardar Patel and Rajendra Babu, no suitable person can be found.

I cannot definitely say who else will be suitable because I am not any more in very close with the Congress organisation.

One thing more. It is also a question as to who should be the President of the Constituent Assembly. I shall not write anything more about it now, because it is not certain whether the Constituent Assembly will meet. Once the Working Committee meeting is over I do not think it is necessary for me to stay on here or at Mussoorie. This hardly needs to be discussed at the Working Committee. Please consider and tell me what I should do. I shall do as you say.

Blessings from

BAPU

[PS.]

*I have a great deal of work to do at Wardha. You may show this whole letter to Maulana Saheb.*

November 5, 1946

CHI. JAWAHARLAL,

The events in Bihar have distressed me. I can clearly see my duty. My bonds with Bihar are close. I cannot forget it. If half of what I hear is true, it means that Bihar has lost all humanity. To say that goondas were responsible for whatever happened there would be quite untrue. Although I have tried hard to avoid the fast, I shall not be able to do so.

It is the seventh day today since I gave up milk and cereals. The cough and the boils were responsible for it, but also I was tired of the body. Then Bihar made matters worse. And the cry came from within: 'Why should you be a witness to this slaughter? If your word, which is as clear as daylight, is not heeded, your work is over. Why do you not die? Such reasoning has forced me to resort to fasting. I want to issue a statement that if in Bihar and other provinces slaughter is not stopped, I must end my life by fasting.

The letter Mohammed Yunus wrote to Shamsuddin is with Sardar Baldev Singh. See it. Is what it says correct? It is our duty to give full report of what happened.

My low diet will continue. There may be delay in undertaking the fast. In Delhi you had asked me about the fast. I had said I had no idea then. Now the situation is not the same. Still you may say what you want to say. If it appeals to me I shall give up the idea of a fast. What I hope is that, knowing my nature, you will appreciate my position. Whatever the issue, I shall advise that all of you continue to do your work. Do not waste time thinking of my death. Leave me in the hands of God and stop worrying.

You can show this letter to the Bihar Cabinet. Is this the Bihar of Brijkishore Prasad?

Blessings from

BAPU

December 30, 1946

CHI. JAWAHARLAL,

Your affection is extraordinary and so natural! Come again, when you wish, or send someone who understands you and will faithfully interpret my reactions when, in your opinion, consultation is necessary and you cannot come. Nor is it seemly that you should often run to me even though I claim to be like a wise father to you, having no less love towards you than Motilalji.

Do not depart from the spirit of the draft you showed me yesterday. . . . Somehow or other I feel that my judgment about the communal problems and the political situation is true. I have no doubt now about the wisdom of what I had said in Delhi when the Working Committee accepted the Cabinet Mission's statement. This does not mean that what was done by the Working Committee should not have been done. On the contrary, I had completely associated myself with all that the Working Committee did. I could not support with reason what I had felt so vaguely.

This time it is quite different. My reason wholly supports my heart. I notice daily verification. So, I suggest frequent consultations with an old, tried servant of the nation.

Blessings from

BAPU

KAZIRKHIL, RAMGANJ P. S.,
NOAKHALI DT.,
February 24, 1947

CHI. JAWAHARLAL,

Today being silence day I am writing this. But it will be typed for your easy reading.

I have read Attlee's speech. Lest I might embarrass you by an untoward word or phrase I am not saying anything just now.

Evidently I had anticipated practically the whole of it in my speeches here, i. e., if I am interpreting the speech correctly. My interpretation is this:

Independence will be recognised of those parts which desired it and will do without British protection.

The British will remain where they are wanted.

This may lead to Pakistan for those provinces or portions which may want it. No one will be forced one way or the other. The Congress provinces if they are wise will get what they want.

Much will depend upon what the Constituent Assembly will do and what you as the Interim Government are able to do.

If the British Government are and are able to remain sincere the declaration is good. Otherwise it is dangerous.

Now about Sardar Niranjan Singh Gill. He has been to Bihar and has produced a report which somewhat reflects upon the Sinha Ministry. You should see him and his report. It has gone to Suhrawardy and Sinha under my advice. He and Sardar Jiwan Singh have not hit it off. The whole thing is bad. I. N. A. seems to have split up. Probably you know all this.

In view of the above report I might have to go to Bihar. God knows. You may show this to friends.

Hope you are well.

Blessings from

BAPU

[PS.]

*I take it that you have a cable from Durban about orders against Drs. Dadoo and Naicker. I trust you have taken prompt action. I have cabled F. M. Smuts.*

June 7, 1947

CHI. JAWAHARLAL,

I had a long conversation with His Excellency. The more I see His Excellency the more I feel that he is sincere. But it is quite possible to damage him if the surrounding atmosphere of which the Indian element is the author overwhelms him, as it may well do any of us.

All the points we discussed at the Working Committee meeting yesterday were touched upon by me and I carried with me the impression that he really appreciated them.

To be wholly truthful requires the highest from of bravery and therefore of non-violence.

Blessings from

BAPU

July 24, 1947

CHI. JAWAHARLAL,

I did not say anything yesterday about the Maulana Saheb. Buy my objection stands. His retiring from the cabinet should not affect our connection with him. There are many positions which he can occupy in public life without any harm to any cause. Sardar is decidedly against his membership in the cabinet and so is Rajkumari. Your cabinet must be strong and effective at the present juncture. It should not be difficult to name another Muslim for the cabinet.

I have destroyed the two copies you sent me yesterday.

Blessings from

BAPU

August 30, 1947

CHI. JAWAHARLAL,

About my going to the Punjab, I won't move without your and Vallabhbhai's wish. I want to say, however, that every day pressure is being put upon me to rush to the Punjab before it is too late. If you wish I could send you all that comes to me so as to enable you to come to the right decision.

If I am not going to the Punjab, would I be of much use in Delhi as an adviser or consultant? I fancy I am not built that way. My advice has value only when I am actually working at a particular thing. I can only disturb when

I give academic advice as on food, clothing, the use of the military. The more I think, the more I sense the truth of this opinion. Left to myself I would probably rush to the Punjab and if necessary break myself in the attempt to stop the warring elements from committing suicide. From a letter I just have from Lord Mountbatten I get the same impression. He would welcome my immediate going to the Punjab.

On this side I have work which must help you all.

Blessings from

BAPU

September 2, 1947

CHI. JAWAHARLAL,

I replied to your message of yesterday.

I would have started for Lahore today but for the flare-up in Calcutta. If the fury did not abate, my going to the Punjab would be of no avail. I would have no self-confidence. If the Calcutta friendship was wrong, how could I hope to affect the situation in the Punjab? Therefore my departure from Calcutta depends solely upon the result of the Calcutta fast. Don't be distressed or angry over the fast.

Blessings from

BAPU

□

# Letters to Vallabh Bhai Patel

Gandhi won freedom for India, while Sardar Patel united the nation. He was a great man possessing strong moral character. He had an uncanny ability to do right thing at the right and ripe moment. It was the secret of his success. Before leaving India, the British freed 562 local and small states in order to further divide the country. But, somehow he made all the states to remain an integral part of India. Only the Nizam of Hyderabad resisted but surrendered before the Indian Army on 13th September 1948. Since then, India grew stronger and remained united.

Sardar Vallabh Bhai Patel was born on 31st October, 1875 in Karamsada village Gujarat. Thaber Bhāi Patel was his father and Lāra Bāi was his mother. They had around 15 acres of land which was enough to feed them. His father had fought against the British as a soldier in the Army of Jhānsi ki Rāni in 1857. Sardar Patel followed him and bravely participated in the struggle for India's Independence under Mahātmā Gandhi.

Patel passed his Matriculation examination at the age of 22 from Nādiād High School. He became a Mukhtar and started his practice at Godharā. He shifted to Boresada where he was very successful.

Once, when Patel was representing a case, he got a telegram that his wife had died. He put the telegram in his pocket and completed the argument then announced her death to his juniors and collegues.

Later on, he went to England and returned back after becoming a barrister. The first thing he did as a freedom fighter was the end of bonded labour in Gujarat. He led from the front the movement of Bardoli. The government behaved in an arrogant manner to suppress the poor peasants but Patel was adamant and won it. The government was forced to reduce the tax. On his grand victory Mahātmā Gandhi gave him the title of "Sardar".

He was arrested many times but released. His longest imprisonment was from August 1942 to June 1945. He represented Congress in the talks for final freedom.

After independence, Patel became the first Home Minister of India. He is still reckoned as the strongest Home Minister ever.

Gandhi and Patel enjoyed a very cordial relationship. They had immense faith in each other.

৪০৫

ON THE TRAIN FROM
POONA TO BOMBAY,
September 15, 1933

BHAI VALLABHBHAI,

I got your letter in the train and I am writing this reply immediately. I am going to Bombay. On Wednesday I will go to Ahmedabad. I have to perform two ceremonies there on Thursday. You must have read about that. I expect to reach Wardha on the 23rd. The programme after that will be decided there.

Don't worry at all about my health. I do take, and will continue to take, the utmost care. I can drink two pounds of milk and eat fruit and vegetables. My weight is 100 pounds. The body is massaged daily. Dr. Dinshaw takes great care of my health. He will come to Bombay also. Premlilabehn literally bathed me in her love. 'Parnakuti' has practically become a second home to me. I am very glad that you have continued honey. Should I ask her to send you some? She will be coming to Bombay tomorrow. She frequently visits the place. Aunt was with me all the time. She is an amazing mixture. There is no doubt about her love, but she always creates difficulties. Jawaharlal's health is excellent. He has still preserved the qualities of character which his name connotes. He will now go to Lucknow. He stayed in 'Parnakuti' with me. He was accompanied by Upadhyaya. Manzar Ali and Professor also were there. Professor had fever, but there is no cause for anxiety. Andrews has remained behind in Poona for two days to have some rest.

Devdhar has become very weak. Write a letter inquiring after his health. Shastri is all right now and has returned to Poona. Most probably Chandrashankar will accompany me on my visits. The only difficulty is about his health. Mathuradas also is accompanying. But it is not certain whether he will come to Wardha. Most probably he will accompany up to there. Mirabehn, of course, will be in the party. Prabhavati also is with me up to now.

I had a long letter from Mahadev. He is fairly well. He reads and spins. Pannalal was in Poona and will now go to Bombay. Kaka also will come to Bombay in two or three days. Ba is quite well. Do the needful about your tooth. Have you kept up the study of Sanskrit? Don't worry about anything. I have written to Mani and told her that, when she is released, she should go and see you and then see me wherever I am. Kamala Nehru has a cardiac ailment. She is in Lucknow. Why should we care whether or not we get any company? Why should one who feels the presence of God need other company? However, you have done right in writing about that, as also about visits. I have to draw up a tour programme for Harijan work in consultation with Ghanshyamdas (Birla) and Thakkar Bapa. Anandi is well on the whole. Narahari's children have been ill for some time.

They are being properly looked after and treated. Bablo has gone to live with his aunt. He went on crying till he had his way.

Nirmala is all right, and so also Sharda. I get letters from Anandi. In Bombay I shall be staying in Mani Bhavan, and in Ahmedabad at Ranchhodbhai's place. Send for anything you want. Mahadev has taken over charge of making envelopes.

Blessings from

BAPU

⊕ ⊕ ⊕

BHAI VALLABHBHAI,

There is a saying in English that great men think alike, and, since both of us are great, we thought alike regarding the cremation rites for Vithalbhai. I have written to Dahyabhai. I am not likely to publish anything as being your view. With regard to the wires and cables which you have received, after informing the Major write one sentence in your next letter to me to the following effect : "On my behalf please thank through the Press all those who have sent letters and wires or cables of condolence." If the Major cannot pass that on his own, he should write to the I. G. and, if he passes it, we shall publish it . . .

Nariman was here yesterday. He took a fairly long time with me and I readily gave it. My warden let me do that. Just now, however, we may pound any amount of paddy we like but we shall get nothing but chaff.

Deenabandhu is arriving here today. He is returning after an extensive tour, and so I expect that he will want much time with me and I shall have to give it.

Kaka's fast will end tomorrow. He is cheerful. He doesn't seem to have been visibly affected by the fast. He doesn't feel a burning sensation [in passing urine] as I do. He can drink plenty of water, no matter whether it is mixed with salt or soda or is hot or cold. If God would grant me the same ability, I should even at this age like to improve upon Bhansali's performance. I wouldn't mind if, in consequence, I became crazy like him. He wears a codpiece of hessian suspended from a string of coir tied round his waist. He eats moistened flour and wanders about. He reappears sometimes in the form of a postcard and tells me in it that he is getting real spiritual experience only now. During the fast, [Kaka] also did some writing through dictation. Prabhudas has become his honorary secretary and also recites from the Gita for him. Since Prabhudas has been Kaka's favourite disciple, the arrangement suits the latter very well. Kishorelal and Gomati also arrived yesterday. I was the cause of their coming.

Kaka has done his duty as friend and father to the best of his ability... continues to follow his own way in his inordinate pride. But I have not given up hope of him. I do believe, though, that his eyes will not open till he stumbles some day. What you say is quite right. A coward's wisdom won't carry him far. On the contrary, if an insolent boy like... who is always flying in the air, became wise, his wisdom would never desert him afterwards and would help him fearlessly to mount the gallows. But that seems too good to come true. I think Kaka will soon regain his strength. Don't worry about him. During the fast, I didn't let my knowledge as a quack rust, so that, over and above the spiritual benefit from the fast, his body has certainly benefited. You did well in administering a powerful dose of medicine to... and Pandya. But the effect of such medicines does not last long and their reactions are sometimes dangerous. I am not saying this to criticise your medicine. My only purpose is to draw your attention to the truth. Mahadev writes to me regularly. He has been collecting books from all sources. I suppose one day all those books will go to a public library. I hope he doesn't go blind in jail through excessive reading. I do intend to send him a mildly-worded prohibitory order. Dr. Datta visited Devdas [in jail]. The latter seems to be making good use of his time. He reads, teaches, plays games and spins. My programme is as follows : Up to the end of this month, the C. P., then Delhi, then the Punjab, then Sind, then Rajputana, then the U. P., Bengal, Assam, etc. This is the plan at present. But it is not impossible that there may be some change in this programme and I may go to Madras earlier. I shall be leaving this place on the 8th. I shall have to come back later for two or three days for a tour of the Wardha taluka. I will write to Deodhar regarding your letter. Rajendrababu has again been removed to a hospital. I think he will now be kept there for some time.

Blessing from

BAPU

August 24, 1935

BHAI VALLABHBHAI,

Andrews has taken ill and, therefore, has stayed on here. . . . Jayakar's reply is enclosed. Preserve it for some time. I have asked him with whom he had the conversation and what it was he found fault with in the administration [of the Tilak Swaraj Fund]. I will send you his reply when it is received. He may act as he wishes.

I send with this a telegram from Devdas. It was something of a shock. I have wired to him and assured him that, if he took complete rest and abstained from food, there was no danger. Raja of course will go. Ba and Manu are already with him. There is also a physician like Ansari to look after him. What more can we desire? I am not worrying at all.

Kumarappa is arriving there today. Do what is necessary about him. I wrote to you about him in yesterday's letter. Let him come back as soon as the examination is over.

Blessings from

BAPU

MY DEAR VALLABHBHAI,

Whatever changes I am making are dictated by your abundant love. I am doing it against my own inclination. This is to tell you that as from today I have been compelled to stop taking service from girls. Lilavati, A. S., etc., have certainly not liked it. Sharada and Vijaya have not liked it either. The last two are sensible and so they are not feeling sad. Prabhavati came yesterday. She may be doing something or the other but even she is looking on in silence. Sushila is continuing to serve me. She has not the heart to stop doing it while I am ill. But I feel that I should stop it when I get well. As from yesterday I have stopped sleeping close to them. That is, the girls sleep far enough to be out of reach of my arms. Sushila hardly slept near me. Now no girl or man sleeps close to me. Sushila spreads her bed perpendicularly at my head. So does Rajkumari near my feet. I am not at all sorry about these changes. Maybe I am unhappy on account of the girls. I say 'maybe' because that is not the impression I get. It is my way to abandon things for the sake of my colleagues. I like to make such sacrifices, because thereby I can know myself better. I know that you have made your suggestion in order to protect me. You have of course considered the interests of the girls. It remains to be seen if their interest will be served by this sacrifice. Lilavati is lying utterly exhausted right now. She is planning to study. I am encouraging her.

If you send this letter to Mahadev, Devdas will also see it.

I have replied to the Viceroy's statement. It is a harsh reply but there was no other alternative. It seems it is going to be a terrible battle. It cannot be predicted how far it will take us. It has to be seen how long my body can take the strain. The swelling is of course reduced. There is silence most of the time. Ba will have left.

Blessings from

BAPU

SEVAGRAM,
February 23, 1942

BHAI VALLABHBHAI,

Mahadev has had a serious attack. Yesterday he left with Ghanshyamdas for a seven-day visit to Nasik, but felt giddy on the way to the station. He, therefore, wisely decided not to proceed further and went to the Civil Surgeon instead. After getting himself treated there for a while, he returned home. He is better now. The bloodpressure has come down to normal. But he had a narrow escape. This is an indication that he needs a long rest. Do not worry. He has the same trouble that Narahari had. He is of course sure to get well.

How are you yourself?

Blessings from

BAPU

[PS.]

*If Prithvi Singh comes to you, give him some time.*

SEVAGRAM,
April 13, 1942

BHAI VALLABHBHAI,

I got a letter from you after many days. I went on writing and dictating letters to Mahadev. But you were stuck in the capital. Never mind. You did well.

I am not surprised to learn that the intestines are not coming round. They do need long rest.

Jawaharlal now seems to have completely abandoned ahimsa. You should go on doing what you can. Restrain the people if you can.

His speech reported today seems terrible. I intend to write to him.

Blessings from

BAPU

SARDAR VALLABHBHAI
68 MARINE DRIVE
BOMBAY

PANCHGANI,
July 17, 1946

BHAI VALLABHBHAI,

I have your letter. I have gone through the speech of the Maharaja of Kashmir. I do not like it. All the same I am quite certain that Jawaharlal should do nothing in haste. He should not go when it suits the Maharaja. It is for us to consider when he should. The Working Committee must meet and discuss it. He should go when the Committee wants him to go. It may also be that the Kashmir affair will be used to sabotage the whole thing. I feel that we should not let such a possibility arise. I hope that whatever is done will be done after the Constituent Assembly meets. I would go so far as to say that the Maulana or you should go there first and find out what is feasible. It may also be necessary for the Maulana to issue a statement addressed to the people of Kashmir. If in spite of all that we do the whole thing collapses it cannot be helped. The situation requires very careful consideration. Munshi will tell you the rest.

Please also see the letter I have written to Jawaharlal.

Blessings from

BAPU

BHAI VALLABHBHAI,

It is 4 a. m. and I am writing this by the light of lantern. All others are asleep and will rise when the electricity comes on at five. So I have only this piece of paper to write on.

I received all your letters. It was a good thing that you met Bhimarao Ambedkar. He will not agree. Why 20 per cent? I see a snag in this. Do think about it. The deposit ought to be paid. One can understand the condition that in all elections a certain minimum number of Harijans should be elected.

I think that the Maharaja's letter about Kashmir is fairly good. I already informed you of the advice I have given and I enclose copies herewith.

I have said that I will see Bhimarao if he comes to Poona or Sevagram. The newspaper report is false.

A great many things seem to be slipping out of the hands of the Congress. The postmen do not listen to it, nor does Ahmedabad, nor do Harijans, nor Muslims. This is a strange situation indeed.

Yesterday, Deo, the Raja of Aundh, Appa etc., came. We had a long discussion. Bhai . . . came with representatives of East Africa. He will meet you. I think something can be done in the matter.

Are you not well enough to go to Ahmedabad? You are ruining your own health. I wish you had come here.

Blessings from

BAPU

SARDAR VALLABHBHAI PATEL
68 MARINE DRIVE
BOMBAY

❀ ❀ ❀

BHAI VALLABHBHAI,

I have your letter... also came and saw me. It will be better if you issue a statement on Goa. You may mention in it that people belonging to various parties have been coming to you for advice and that it is risky for them to have so many parties. They must all speak with one voice; and they should not build their hopes on people from outside Goa. Too many statements are likely to make for confusion. It will therefore be better if everything is sent to the Bombay Congress Committee and then an official statement is issued by it. As I see it, the present struggle in Goa is only for civil liberty and it must succeed. Although the whole of India sympathises with it the hardships will have to be borne by the Indians in Goa. Goa's freedom is bound to follow India's freedom. There is little perhaps the people of Goa need do for that today.

I understand about Bhimarao. Do see him. His speeches are in bad taste. It would be good if you answered the two points he has made. I do not have figures about the elections and caste Hindus; I am getting them.

I do not agree with you at all about your health. You must do something about it. It is a pity you have no confidence at all in Dinshaw, but there are many others. In any case you must not allow your health to get worse.

I understand about Ahmedabad. There is no question of your going there when people themselves do not want it.

Blessings from

BAPU

91

BHAI VALLABHBHAI,

I received your letter. Immediately I sat down to write to Abidali. Nobody can forcibly lodge in the Congress House. And how can they resort to fasting?

I understand about Jawaharlal. For the moment everything is going to come off without a hitch. About the future we shall see.

Pyarelal tells me that there is a newspaper report about the meeting of the Working Committee in Wardha on the 8th.

You must have heard about Munshi's visit to Delhi. The situation is becoming more and more delicate.

There are other strikes on top of the postal strike. All this looks pretty significant. It is necessary that you and others should think about it very seriously. The Congress position may seem strong on the surface but it appears to have lost its hold on the people. Or it may be that the Congress itself is involved in these troubles if only from a distance. This must be clarified; otherwise the battle which we are on the point of winning will be lost.

I hope you are well. These days it has been raining here all the twenty-four hours.

Blessings from

BAPU

PANCHGANI,
July 27, 1946

BHAI VALLABHBHAI,

I have your letter. Sudhir cannot refuse to go now. If Jinnah Saheb's man is also going, let him go. I think in the letter I wrote him I must have said that the Cabinet would welcome it if he also sent someone. Be it as it may, if there is time it would be as well if Sudhir meets you and me before he leaves. It is certainly necessary to think carefully over all that is happening, but it is no use worrying about it. I have not yet received Sudhir's letter; if I had, I would have sent it on to you at once.

I have already written a letter to Abidali which he must have received the night before last or yesterday morning. I feel that if Abidali does not leave the Congress House, Congress officials should start satyagraha against him. That is, they can give him notice and then vacate and lock up all the rooms in the Congress House until he leaves. If such satyagraha is not possible, they should give him notice of trespass and ask him to leave.

I will leave Poona on the 5th or the 6th. I wish to go to Wardha. I have purposely decided to entrain at Kalyan. In that case there is no need to go to Bombay. I do not like living under police guard and putting my host and all others to inconvenience. I had told the overseer all this. I had told Lilavati, too, and most probably Patil also. Nor would I like staying anywhere else. You agree with all this, don't you?

Blessings from

BAPU

POONA,
August 1, 1946

BHAI VALLABHBHAI,

I have not been able to answer your letter fully. The main problem is about Ambedkar. I see a risk in coming to any sort of understanding with him, for he has told me in so many words that for him there is no distinction between truth and untruth or between violence and non-violence. He follows one single principle, viz., to adopt any means which will serve his purpose. One has to be very careful indeed when dealing with a man who would become a Christian, Muslim or Sikh and then be reconverted according to his convenience. There is much more I could write in the same strain. To my mind it is all a snare. It is a "catch". Besides, it is not necessary for him at present to insist on 20 p. c. If India becomes independent in the real sense—the provinces to some extent are— and if the caste Hindus are true to themselves, all will be well. But if the number of fair-minded persons is small and if power passes into the hands of fanatics, there is bound to be injustice, no matter what agreements you make today. You may come to any understanding you like today— but who are the people who beat up Harijans, murder them, prevent them from using public wells, drive them out of schools and refuse them entry into their homes? They are Congressmen. Aren't they? It is very necessary to have a clear picture of this. I therefore feel that at present we should not insist on an agreement such as you suggest. However, we should stress the capacity of the Congress to do justice. Mine may be a voice in the wilderness. Even so I prefer it that way. Therefore, if we negotiate with Ambedkar out of fear of the League we are likely to lose on both the fronts.

I will definitely leave here on the 5th and reach Wardha on the 6th. I have already written to you and informed you that I have deliberately decided not to go to Bombay and I adhere to that decision. But if you want it to be modified, do tell me by all means— that means I shall have to remain in a railway compartment for a few hours more. You may see me there if necessary but in any case not at the cost of your health. There is nothing we cannot deal with through correspondence. In any case do come to Wardha on the 8th. You may come even a day earlier if you like.

If postmen are using high-handed methods, I think it will be perfectly proper to raise our voice against it.

Blessings from

BAPU

BHAI VALLABHBHAI,

I am enclosing a copy of my letter to Jawaharlal, which please see. I have nothing more to say. If you have anything to say, do let me know. I am willing to listen. This fast is not like the ones you have witnessed, though it is not too different either. I have passed through no small agony.

Rajaji, Devdas and others should read this letter.

No one should come rushing to me. There are so many to assist me. My going on living depends entirely on complete peace being established in India. You will certainly do everything to achieve that end. Do not attach too much weight to the warnings about my death. Say rather that if I have erred, there will be no harm in letting me die. I am well.

Blessings from

BAPU

DATTAPARA,
November 14, 1946

CHI. VALLABHBHAI,

I began with 'Chi'. and therefore do not score it out to make 'Bhai'. You are to me what you are. Acharya told me everything. I have communicated my view to Jawaharlal. Please see it. The more I think about it, the more I find myself against the Congress session at Meerut. It is best not to have a session, but if you must have one, have it in New Delhi. Since it is Kripalani's affair, it is only right to let him take the final decision, though everyone should give his own view. His address may be printed and read if the Congress is called off. You have many problems before you. You need peace to be able to solve them. You need time as well. If a mistake is made now, it will prove to be very costly.

I cannot leave this place. If it is necessary to consult me, you should come here and ask me. That is the only way out. Truly speaking, there should be no need at all to consult me. I have said and done enough. The work here may perhaps be my last. If I survive this, it will be a new life for me. My non-violence is being tested here in a way it has never been tested before.

I hope you are all well enough to be able to work.

❀   ❀   ❀

SRIRAMPUR,
December 4, 1946

CHI. VALLABHBHAI,

Herewith a statement of my views about the Constituent Assembly. Please go through it and do what you think fit. Jawaharlal's absence will be a handicap. I hold very strong views in the matter. There is certainly no weakness on our part in giving up the plan. Doing what the situation demands is no weakness. But maybe I am quite wrong.

Blessings from

BAPU

❀   ❀   ❀

SRIRAMPUR,
December 25, 1946

CHI. VALLABHBHAI,

Your letter addressed to Pyarelal reached me direct yesterday. Pyarelal and all the rest are engrossed in their own duties and are staking their lives. He could, when we were together at one place, write or send you something. He cannot do so now. Your letter went to Kazirkhil; so Satis Babu forwarded it to me here. Pyarelal does not know about your letter. He comes to see me occasionally and will read it when he comes here next.

I am dictating this at 3 a.m. I shall have a wash at 4 a.m. and prayers after that. This is the present routine. I shall carry on only if such is God's will. However, there is no need to worry about my health. The body responds to the demands made upon it, but I am being tested. My truth and non-violence are being weighed in a balance which is much more accurate than any pearl merchant ever used. It is so sensitive as to register the difference of even a hundredth fraction of a hair. Truth and non-violence themselves can never be imperfect. If anything is to be found wanting, it may be I who have constituted myself their representative; if so, I at least hope that God will take me away and work through some other agent. I am sorry that I cannot myself do the work which Pyarelal used to do for me and I have not yet been able to arrange with the two men who are with me to do it. But both are intelligent. I therefore hope to be able to arrange it. In this, your letter will afford me encouragement. Jaisukhlal left Manu here at her own wish three or four days ago. I allowed her to come and stay with me on her terms, as she was prepared to live and die with me if necessary. And now I am dictating this to her, lying with my eyes closed so as to avoid strain. Sucheta is also in the room. She is still asleep and I am dictating this letter in a low voice, lying on the wooden bedstead. The bedstead is of a size on which three persons can easily sleep. I do all my work on it. The telegram you have forwarded to me has no substance. There is no limit to exaggeration here. Not that people exaggerate intentionally; they simply do not know what exaggeration means. The imagination of the people runs riot like the local vegetation which grows like grass on all sides. All around us I find huge coconut and betelnut palms, and a large variety of greens grow in their shade. The rivers are all [big] like the Indus, the Ganges, the Jumna and the Brahmaputra. They empty their waters into the Bay of Bengal. My advice is that if you have not already replied to the correspondent who sent you the telegram, you should ask him to furnish proof for his statements so that the Central Government may try to do something about it though they have no power to interfere in terms of the Constitution. And add: 'Gandhi is there in your midst and it is impossible that he would not listen to you. But he is an apostle of truth and non-violence and it is therefore likely that you are disappointed with him. But if he disappoints you, how can we, who were trained under him, hope to satisfy you ? But we shall do what we can.' Don't tell anyone that since I am here, he need not bring his problems to you. Tell him that he may write to you nevertheless and that it will be your duty to afford relief to him even by going against me, for that is what I have taught you.

The situation here poses many difficulties and problems. Truth is nowhere to be found. Violence masquerades as non- violence and heinous crimes are committed in the name of religion. But truth and non-violence can be tested only in such conditions. I know this and that is why I am here. Do not send for me. If I run away from cowardice that will be my own misfortune; but I do not yet see such a misfortune befalling the country. I am here to do or die. News came over the radio yesterday that Jawaharlal, Kripalani and Deo are coming to have consultations with me. That is good. What is the use of my meeting everyone? However, if anyone among you wants to ask me anything, he is welcome. What I wrote about Assam was not meant for immediate publication. If you know how it came to be published, please let me know. But rest assured that I am right on that point. I am in the furnace here. I, therefore, am in a good enough position to testify what is happening in it and what the truth is. [Sardar Jivan Singh] often comes to me, asks for suggestions and assures me that he will implement them to the letter. I think I can trust him. I had a wire from [Sardar Niranjan Singh] saying that he had not been able to win you over. But I did not understand what he actually meant. Tell him this if he is there and if you happen to meet him. And if you have been able to understand what he wants to ask me, let me know.

You will have seen the report of the Bihar [Muslim] League. I have written to Rajendra Babu about it and have asked him to acquaint all of you with my views. I have written to the Chief Minister also. It is dreadful even if half of it is true. I have no doubt at all that an impartial commission of inquiry, which is above reproach, should be immediately set up. There should not be delay of even a single day. Whatever is true in the allegations must be admitted straight away and the rest should be referred to the commission. Discuss this with your Muslim League colleagues in the Cabinet also. I am in correspondence with Suhrawardy. It is continuing. I will send it all to you when it is completed. Jawahar and others will see what has passed between us so far. If you are not doing so already, please read the summaries of my postprayer speeches which are sent to the newspapers. Or go through the cuttings which Mani may give you. I know even from here the great pressure under which you are working, but there are certain things which have got to be done despite the pressure. To keep yourself informed of what I say, is one of them.

How can I say you will be well? I will assume that you are well enough to carry on the work. I am sure you can improve your health. I would still advise you to send for Dinshaw . I have no doubt that he is a good and a sincere man with an altruistic outlook. What if he is not so efficient? You ask about Sushila . I cannot say that she is in very good health. She too is in an inhospitable village and is doing good work. Even a quack is a rarity in these parts; so naturally people make much of someone like her. Do not, therefore, be anxious for any of us here. And when everyone of them is here, ready to die, their falling ill should be of no great concern. If one dies, it is as well; only let the death be pure and earn commendation.

Blessings from

BAPU

CHI. VALLABHBHAI,

I have your letter. Jawahar and others will be able to tell you about what happened here.

I hold strong views about. . . . The work being done here cannot be carried on with the Congress funds or funds collected by you. He should collect the money publicly both from Hindus and Muslims. I am also getting more convinced from experience that all activities which are carried on with the help of money alone are sure to fail. You also should give up any idea of getting things done with money. It is essential that . . . should not deviate even an inch from what is agreed to between him and me. I am resolved that I will get out of it as soon as I see even the slightest impurity. This mission is most delicate and the biggest that has fallen to my lot. God has sustained me so far. I wake up and start work at 1.30 a. m., standard time, and there has been no difficulty yet. About tomorrow, God alone knows.

I have heard many complaints against you. If there is any exaggeration in "many", it is unintended. Your speeches tend to be inflammatory and play to the gallery. You have lost sight of all distinction between violence and non-violence. You are teaching the people to meet violence with violence. You miss no opportunity to insult the Muslim League in season and out of season. If all this is true, it is very harmful. They say you talk about holding on to office. That also is disturbing, if true. Whatever I heard I have passed on to you for you to think over. The times are very critical. If we stray from the straight and narrow path by ever so little, we are done for. The Working Committee does not function harmoniously as it should. Root out corruption; you know how to do it. If you feel like it, send some sensible and reliable person to explain things to me and understand my point of view. There is no need whatever for you to rush down here. You are no longer fit to run about. It is not good that you do not take care of your health. I will stop here. It is now 5.35, Calcutta time, and there are heaps of arrears to be disposed of.

Blessings from

BAPU

DALTA,
January 24, 1947

CHI. VALLABHBHAI,

I have both your letters. I am dictating this while spinning. A messenger has come and I must send this with him. I get no information about what is happening in other parts of the country. I had heard about Hazara and so I sent the wire. The work here takes up all my time. It is no easy matter to change one's house daily. God has somehow sustained me so far. Let us see what he does now. The poison [of communalism] is public knowledge. Non-violence has to make its way through it. That is the only way in which it can be put to the test.

The letter from the Nawab of Bhopal contains nothing new. He has not answered my question. Notes were taken of my conversation with him when I was in Delhi. I did not have a copy, and he has now sent one. I have not read them, but I assume that they are all right. The question which I had put to him is bound to come up.

I was glad to learn that your health was better and that you had called in a naturopath though not Dinshaw. In my view, nature cure is the only thing for you.

Parasuram the typist has left. His departure has made no difference. He has lost his balance. But I do not need any substitute.

Blessings from

BAPU

101

CHI. VALLABHBHAI,

I got your letter. I made a long speech about the League. A report of it has been sent to the Press. You may have read it in the newspapers. It summarises my views on the subject.

I take the Cabinet Mission statement to mean that there is nothing to fear even if the Princes do not join the Constituent Assembly. Nothing will be lost even if they do not interpret it in the same way. And if they do, it will only be worthy of them and we shall be able to work without obstruction. It is as clear as daylight to me that there is no need to put up with shortages in food and cloth. It is another matter if I cannot convince others about it. In such circumstances it makes no difference whether or not I come there. My place is here only. I am satisfied with what I can do here. I believe that I am bringing some little solace to the people here and may be able to bring more if I continue the work. But that is in the hands of Providence.

I hear that your opposition is reported to be the reason why the Bihar Ministry does not appoint an inquiry commission. I do not believe the story, but I bring it to your notice. If a commission is not appointed, it will do great harm. The Ministry will be regarded as guilty. If their work has been above board, what harm can the Commission do to them? Considerable pressure is being exerted on me, but I do not go because I have reposed confidence in the Ministers. But if a Commission is not appointed after all, I shall have no choice but to go to Bihar.

I hope you are taking sufficient care of your health.

Blessings from

BAPU

SARDAR VALLABHBHAI
HOME MINISTER, NEW DELHI

102

CHI. VALLABHBHAI,

I forgot to ask you one thing. I could not find the time. I now see that I must write something in *Harijan* . . . I also notice that there are frequent differences between your approach and mine. Such being the case, would it be advisable for me to meet the Viceroy even as an individual?

Please think over this objectively, keeping only the good of the country in view. If you like, you may discuss the matter with others. Please do not see the slightest suggestion of a complaint from me in this. I am thinking of my duty in terms of the country's good. It is quite possible that what you can see while administering the affairs of millions may not be realized by me. If I were in the place of you all, I would perhaps say and do exactly what you are saying and doing.

Blessings from

BAPU

SARDAR VALLABHBHAI PATEL
1 AURANGZEB ROAD
NEW DELHI

VALMIKI MANDIR
NEW DELHI,
June 23, 1947

CHI. VALLABHBHAI,

The news today is the limit. Look at the Reuters cable. The Bill provides for two nations. What then is the point of the big talks going on here? If there has been no tacit acceptance on our part you people can prevent this crime.

Once the Bill is passed, no one will listen to you.

In my opinion [Ravishankar Shukla]'s speech was certainly bad. That he said what he did in jest does not take away from the gravity of the lapse. I personally feel that he should be asked to resign only if he is also guilty of some other lapse. To dismiss him solely on this ground will be difficult.

I have also written to Jawaharlal about this.

Blessings from

BAPU

SARDAR VALLABHBHAI PATEL
1, AURANGZEB ROAD
NEW DELHI

❀   ❀   ❀

VALMIKI MANDIR,
NEW DELHI,
July 24, 1947

CHI. VALLABHBHAI,

The more I think of it the more I am convinced that I should leave here as soon as the Kashmir affair is settled. I do not like much of what is going on. I do not say that for that reason it should be changed; but only that I should not be said to be associated with it. Moreover, I must reach Bihar and thence Noakhali before the 15th. That too is urgent work. I would request you not to detain me any more. There are still four or five days in any case.

I even feel that *Harijan* should now be stopped. I do not like leading the country in an opposite direction. Please think over all this when you have time.

Blessings from

BAPU

SARDAR VALLABHBHAI PATEL
1 AURANGZEB ROAD
NEW DELHI

❀   ❀   ❀

104

CHI. VALLABHBHAI,

Two Khaksars came to see me yesterday. One of them wept bitterly. The other complained that although an official had assured them that now nothing would be done to them since they were going away, yet there was firing in the mosque the same evening, that many were killed, that an old man of seventy received seven bullets, that no one knew how many had died and how many had survived and that for three days the Khaksars were kept there without food and water, unable even to go out to answer calls of nature.

I was stunned to hear all this. I rebuked them. I said it could not be true. I said, "Sardar told me only today that since the Khaksars would not leave the mosque, police officials had to enter the mosque, that they did so with the permission of the Imam, that the action that was taken was ordered by the Muslim officer, that no violence had been used, nothing beyond tear-gas had been fired and that no one had been killed. I therefore cannot swallow what you say." They answered, "If that is what your Sardar says, how can we hope to be believed? What use asking for justice now? One day you will know. Truth will be out." I said, "If I hear of a wrong being done I do not hide it even for the sake of my dear ones. I shall say no more. I will do my duty." Now if there is anything in this please let me know.

Blessings from

BAPU

SARDAR VALLABHBHAI PATEL
1, AURANGZEB ROAD
NEW DELHI

CHI. VALLABHBHAI,

I have already written to you—haven't I—that I do not wish to go to Kashmir and that Jawaharlal will go instead. Now I have a letter from the Viceroy saying I may go but not Jawaharlal. I therefore cannot make up my mind. What shall I do?

Blessings from

BAPU

❀ ❀ ❀

LAHORE,
August 6, 1947

SARDAR SAHEB,

I am giving this note to the Khaksar friends who had met me there. They complain of further injustice. They had left their luggage in a hotel and come to see me. The police took away their luggage in their absence. I told them I could do no more than write and enquire. They said: "No one would listen to us. Give us a letter so that someone may give us a patient hearing, after that what is ordained will happen." They say they desire nothing except to serve the people. I am not asking you to hear them yourself. It should be enough if you ask some official to hear their complaint.

Please send me a reply to my earlier letter on the subject.

Blessings from

BAPU

❀ ❀ ❀

LAHORE,
August 6, 1947

CHI. VALLABHBHAI,

I am sending a note to Jawaharlal. He will show it to you.

106

Kaka has written a letter to the Maharaja. He will be sending you a copy of it. He has shown it to me. He has a sweet tongue. I had an hour's talk with the Maharaja and Maharani. He agreed that only what the subjects want should be done. But he did not say anything about the main thing. He therefore sent his private secretary to express his regrets. The thing is that he wants to get rid of Kaka. He has been deliberating on how he can do it. It had almost been decided to appoint Sir Jaylal. I think you should do something in the matter. In my opinion, the situation in Kashmir can be saved.

The work done in the Wah Camp is quite good. The people ought not to be removed from there. You should take up this matter with the Pakistan Government. Hindus and Sikhs should be rehabilitated in Rawalpindi. Read the speeches I have made in the Punja Saheb and Wah Camp. I have made that suggestion. I am staying with Rameshwari Nehru here and am leaving in the evening by the Calcutta Mail. I will stop in Patna for a day and then proceed to Calcutta and Noakhali.

As I felt it was necessary I have left behind Sushila in the Camp. The people welcome it. They are in great panic but I see no reason for it.

I hope you are taking care of your health.

Blessings from

BAPU

BELIAGHATA,
August 30, 1947

CHI. VALLABHBHAI,

I have your letter. I have received from Jawahar also a telegram similar to what you have sent. My reply is contained in the accompanying letter. I therefore do not write more here.

May God give all of you the strength and the wisdom the situation demands. Did you ever think that you would have to face such a difficult situation so soon? His will be done.

Horace is with me.

Blessings from

BAPU

CALCUTTA,
September 1, 1947

CHI. VALLABHBHAI,

I got your letter. Bhopal (Nawab's) letter is strange. I did not like it. Your task is hard indeed. May God grant you the necessary strength. If Bhopal plays the game, Hyderabad's problem will be easy to solve. And the same will be true of Pakistan.

I have already sent you my programme, but now even that is as good as cancelled. We were to go to Noakhali tomorrow morning. So Shaheed Saheb went home. I am the only elderly person in the house. Dinshaw Mehta is here, but what can he do? He does not know the language and his large body is of no use.

Someone received knife wounds in Machhva Bazaar. No one knew who stabbed him. People brought him here for demonstration. Perhaps they wanted to attack Shaheed Suhrawardy, but they could not find him; so their anger was turned on me. There was an uproar in the front yard. Both the girls went out among the crowd. I was in bed about to go to sleep. Our Muslim landlady came in to have a look as she was afraid I might come to harm. I sensed danger and got up. I broke my silence. My vow permits me to break it on such occasions. I went to face the crowd but the girls would not leave my side. Other people also surrounded me. Glass windows were being broken and they started smashing the doors also. There was an attempt to cut the wires of the electric ceiling fans but only a few were snapped. I started shouting at the crowd, asking them to be quiet. But who would listen? I could, moreover, speak only Hindustani and they were Bengalis. There were also some Muslims nearby. I asked them not to strike back. So they merely stood around me. There were two groups; one trying to incite the crowd, the other trying to pacify it. There were two policemen also. They also used no force. With folded hands they addressed [the crowd] in a loud voice and they stopped me. Kalyanam suggested that I should go and sit inside. Bisen was in the centre. He was wearing only pyjamas and was taken for a Muslim. Bricks were thrown. One hit a Muslim. No one was wounded, but the brick could have struck me. The Superintendent of Police came soon after and the youngsters dispersed after causing considerable damage to the house. Prafulla Babu and Annada arrived. Prafulla suggested the posting of more police guard but I objected. Everyone suspects the Hindu Mahasabha [was behind the attack]. I have asked them to see Syamaprasad and Chatterji before arresting the mischief-makers and not to do anything in a hurry. Such is the position here. I could thus go to bed only at 12.30 a. m. Of course I had to get up at the usual hour.

Please tell Jawaharlal about this when you meet him.

Read the accompanying wire. I feel totally lost. I pin my hopes on you two. The copy of my reply is on the reverse.

In this situation you may take it that I am here. "As for tomorrow, who can tell?"

Blessings from

BAPU

SARDAR VALLABHBHAI PATEL
1 AURANGZEB ROAD
NEW DELHI

CALCUTTA,<br>
September 1/2, 1947

CHI. VALLABHBHAI,

Today here they are preparing to fight. I have just returned after seeing the dead bodies of two Muslims who had died of wounds. I hear that riots have broken out in many places. Thus what was regarded as a miracle has proved a short-lived nine-day wonder. Now I am thinking what my duty is in the circumstances. I am writing this at about 6 p. m. As the post will go only tomorrow, I shall be able to add something more. Jawahar wires that I should go to the Punjab. But how can I leave Calcutta now? I am thinking within myself and silence helps in that. See the accompanying wire from Mirpur Khas. What could it mean? I have not replied.

*4.45 a. m., September 2, 1947*

This much was written last evening. After that I heard much more. A number of people came to see me. I went on thinking of my own duty. The news I received settled it and I decided to undertake a fast. It began at 8.15 last evening.

BIRLA HOUSE,<br>
NEW DELHI<br>
November 1, 1947

CHI. VALLABHBHAI,

When you came to see me yesterday, I simply forgot that it was your birthday. I could not, therefore give you my blessings personally. Such is my plight today.

I write this for special reasons:

1. Refugees are crowding near the Birla Mandir. It is not possible for all of them to live there and they huddle together somehow. They must be removed to a camp and that too quickly.

2. I enclose a letter regarding mosques. It is only one of many such. A statement should be issued that all of them will be protected from abuse and whatever

damage they might have suffered will be repaired by the Government.

3. It should be announced that those who were forcibly converted to Hinduism or Sikhism will be regarded by the Government as not having changed their religion and will receive adequate protection.

4. No Muslim will be forced to leave the Union.

5. Those who have been compelled to vacate their houses or whose houses have been illegally occupied by others, should be assured that such occupation will be regarded as null and void and that the houses will be reserved for the original owners.

I think it is necessary to issue such a statement.

Blessings from

BAPU

□

# Letters to Muhammad Ali Jinnah

Muhammad Ali Jinnah was initially committed to Hindu-Muslim unity leading Congressmen for several years but in 1913 he joined Muslim League that metamorphosed him into a hardcore Muslim. He gave the idea of two nations and partition, and remained adamant on his demand. He was the founder and first Governor-General of Pakistan. He was fondly called Qāide-Āzam.

Jinnah was born on 25th December, 1876, and died on 11th September 1948, both at Karāchi. He was educated in Mumbai and London. He became a lawyer at the age of 19. After returning to India, he practised law. He was elected to India Imperial Legislative Council in 1910.

Jinnah's reputation as a lawyer in Mumbai became formidable. Ollivant, a Judicial Member, hired him for Rs. 1,500/- per month, which Jinnah refused. Once, he was interrupted thrice by a Judge, during a hearing. On all the three occasions, the Judge said, "Rubbish". Jinnah said ironically, "Nothing but rubbish has passed from your Lordship's mouth throughout the day."

Jinnah was opposed also to Gandhi's Non-cooperation Movement and left congress to join hands with Muslim League. During the late 1920s and early 30s, he was called a moderate Muslim leader by the Muslims, and too Muslim by others. He refused to form government in the provinces with the Congress, and worked solely for the formation of Pakistan, a Muslim State.

Regarding each delicate issue, for example the relation of Gandhi and Jinnah, Jinnah and partition of the country, the facts should be presented as they are and it should be left to the people or the readers to draw their own specific conclusions.

In the following pages, there are as many as 18 letters addressed to M.A. Jinnah, written by Gandhi. The letters speak volumes, and show the situation and different approaches truthfully. Let the letters in general and the letters of the letters' in particular speak directly. They will unravel the reality into the events that eventually and finally came to the night or day of freedom, and resulted in the partition of the country.

ॐ

BOMBAY,
June 28, 1919

DEAR MR. JINNAH,

I was delighted to receive your letter. I shall certainly keep you informed of the doings here. I cannot say anything about the Reforms Bill. I have hardly studied it. My preoccupation is Rowlatt legislation; add to that the Punjab, Kalinath Roy, Transvaal and swadeshi and I have more hay on my work than I can carry. Our Reforms will be practically worthless, if we cannot repeal Rowlatt legislation, if a strong committee of enquiry is not appointed to investigate the Punjab affairs and to revise what appear to be excessive sentences, if the glaring wrong done to Kalinath Roy is not redressed and the Transvaal Indians not protected from further encroachments on their liberty, and if India does not take up and appreciate the work of swadeshi. The first four are needed as much to test our strength as to test the measure of the goodwill of Englishmen, and the last, viz., swadeshi, is an earnest of our love for our country, and I am, therefore, concentrating all my energy upon these things. And as I can imagine no form of resistance to the Government than civil disobedience, I propose, God willing, to resume it next week. I have taken all precautions, that are humanly

113

possible to take, against recrudescence of violence. I have duly informed the authorities of my intentions and I have even sent a cable to Mr. Montagu.

I enclose proof copy of the instructions I shall be leaving behind. They will give you the further information I should like you to possess.

Pray tell Mrs. Jinnah that I shall expect her on her return to join the hand-spinning class that Mrs. Banker Senior and Mrs. Ramabai, a Punjabi lady, are conducting. And, of course, I have your promise that you would take up Gujarati and Hindi as quickly as possible. May I then suggest that like Macaulay you learn at least one of these languages on your return voyage ? You will not have Macaulay's time during the voyage, i.e., six months, but then you have not the same difficulty that Macaulay had. I hope you will both keep well during your stay.

If you get the time, please turn over the pages of *Young India* sent under separate cover. It is wretchedly printed because I have no trained help yet, and I am training helpers at the expense of indulgent subscribers.

Yours sincerely,

M. K. GANDHI

TITHAL,<br>May 22, 1937

DEAR SHRI JINNAH,

Mr. Kher has given me your message. I wish I could do something, but I am utterly helpless. My faith in unity is as bright as ever; only I see no daylight out of the impenetrable darkness and, in such distress, I cry out to God for light.

Your sincerely,

M.K. GANDHI

SEGAON, WARDHA,
October 19, 1937

DEAR FRIEND,

I carefully went through your speech at Lucknow, and I felt deeply hurt over your misunderstanding of my attitude. My letter was in answer to a specially private message you had sent to me. It represented my deepest feeling. The letter was purely personal. Were you right in using it as you did?

Of course, as I read it, the whole of your speech is a declaration of war. Only I had hoped you would reserve poor me as bridge between the two. I see that you want no bridge. I am sorry. Only it takes two to make a quarrel. You won't find me one, even if I cannot become a peace-maker.

This is not for publication, unless you desire it. It is written in all good faith and out of an anguished heart.

Yours sincerely,

M. K. GANDHI

SEGAON, WARDHA,
February 3, 1938

DEAR MR. JINNAH,

Pandit Jawaharlal Nehru told me yesterday that you were complaining to the Maulana Sahib about the absence of any reply from me to your letter of 5th November in reply to one of 19th October. The letter was received by me when I was pronounced by the doctors to be seriously ill in Calcutta. The letter was shown to me three days after its receipt. Had I thought it necessarily called for a reply, even though I was ill I would have sent one. I have re-read the letter. I still think that there was nothing useful that I could have said in reply. But, in a way, I am glad that you awaited a reply. Here it is.

Mr. Kher told me definitely that he had a private message from you. He delivered it to me when I was alone. I could have sent you a verbal message in reply, but in order to give you a true picture of my mental state I sent you the short note. There was nothing to hide in it. But I did feel, as I still do, that the way in which you used it came upon me as a painful surprise.

You complain of my silence. The reason for my silence is literally and truly in my note. Believe me, the moment I can do something that can bring the two communities together nothing in the world can prevent me from so doing.

You seem to deny that your speech was a declaration of war, but your latter pronouncements too confirm the first impression. How can I prove what is a matter of feeling? In your speeches I miss the old nationalist. When in 1915 I returned from the self-imposed exile in South Africa, everybody spoke of you as one of the staunchest of nationalists and the hope of both Hindus and Mussalmans. Are you still the same Mr. Jinnah? If you say you are, in spite of your speeches I shall accept your word.

Lastly, you want me to come forward with some proposal. What proposal can I make except to ask you on bended knees to be what I had thought you were. But the proposal to form a basis of unity between the two communities has surely got to come from you.

This is again not for publication but for your eyes. It is the cry of a friend, not of an opponent.

Yours sincerely,

M. K. GANDHI

DETENTION CAMP,
May 4, 1943

DEAR QAID-E-AZAM,

When some time after my incarceration the Government asked me for a list of newspapers I would like to have, I included the *Dawn* in my list. I have been receiving it with more or less regularity. Whenever it comes to me, I read it carefully. I have followed the proceedings of the League as reported in the *Dawn* columns. I noted your invitation to me to write to you. Hence this letter.

I welcome your invitation. I suggest our meeting face to face rather than talking through correspondence. But I am in your hands.

I hope that this letter will be sent to you and, if you agree to my proposal, that the Government will let you visit me.

One thing I had better mention. There seems to be an "if" about your invitation. Do you say I should write only if I have changed my heart? God alone knows men's hearts. I would like you to take me as I am.

Why should not both you and I approach the great question of communal unity as men determined on finding a common solution, and work together to make our solution acceptable to all who are concerned with it or are interested in it?

Yours sincerely,

M. K. GANDHI

QAID-E-AZAM M. A. JINNAH
MOUNT PLEASANT ROAD
BOMBAY

August 18, 1944

BHAI JINNAH,

How was it you fell ill all of a sudden? The whole world was looking forward to our meeting. I had entertained high hopes, although, I must admit, I had my own apprehensions. Hence when Fatima Behn conveyed to me the news of your illness, I was shaken. I hope God will soon restore you to health, hasten the meeting to which the whole world is looking forward and that the meeting will lead to the welfare of India.

I hope Fatima Behn or someone else will keep me informed about your health.

Your brother,

M. K. GANDHI

DEAR QUAID-E-AZAM,

I have your letter of the 13th instant. I understood from our talks that you were in no hurry for my answer. I was, therefore, taking the matter in a leisurely fashion, even hoping that as our talks proceeded and as cordiality increased, mutual clarification would come of itself and that we would only have to record our final agreement. But I understand and appreciate the other viewpoint. We should take nothing for granted. I should clarify your difficulties in understanding the Rajaji Formula and you should do likewise regarding yours, i.e., the Muslim League Lahore Resolution of 1940.

With reference to the Lahore Resolution, as agreed between us I shall deal with it in a separate letter.

Perhaps at the end of our discussion, we shall discover that Rajaji not only has not put the Lahore Resolution out of shape and mutilated it but has given it substance and form.

Indeed, in view of your dislike of the Rajaji Formula, I have, at any rate for the moment, put it out of my mind and I am concentrating on the Lahore Resolution in the hope of finding a ground for mutual agreement.

So much for the first paragraph of your letter.

As to the second, I do hold that unless we oust the third party we shall not be able to live at peace with one another. That does not mean that I may not make an effort to find ways and means of establishing a living peace between us.

118

You ask for my conception of the basis for a provisional interim government. I would have told you if I had any scheme in mind. I imagine that if we two can agree it would be for us to consult the other parties. I can say this, that any provisional government to inspire confidence at the present moment must represent all parties. When that moment arrives, I shall have been replaced by some authoritative person, though you will have me always at your beck and call when you have converted me or I you, or by mutual conversion we have become one mind functioning through two bodies.

As to the third point, the provisional government, being the appointing authority, will give effect to the findings of the Commission. This I thought was implied in my previous answer.

Rajaji tells me that 'absolute majority' is used in his Formula in the same sense as it is used in ordinary legal parlance wherever more than two groups are dealt with. I cling to my own answer. But you will perhaps suggest a third meaning and persuade me to accept it.

The form of the plebiscite and franchise must be left to be decided by the provisional interim government unless we decide it now. I should say it should be by adult suffrage of all the inhabitants of the Pakistan area.

As to the fourth, 'all parties' means you and I and everyone else holding views on the question at issue will and should seek by peaceful persuasion to influence public opinion as is done where democracy functions wholly or in part.

As to the fifth, supposing that the result of the plebiscite is in favour of partition, the provisional government will draft the treaty and agreements as regards the administration of matters of common interest, but the same has to be confirmed and ratified by the governments of the two States. The machinery required for the settlement and administration of matters of common interest will, in the first instance, be planned by the interim government, but subsequently will be matter for settlement between the two governments acting through the agencies appointed by each for that purpose.

As to the sixth, I hope the foregoing makes superfluous any further reply.

Yours sincerely,

M. K. GANDHI

DEAR QUAID-E-AZAM,

This is in terms of our talks of Wednesday the 13th instant.

For the moment I have shunted the Rajaji Formula and with your assistance am applying my mind very seriously to the famous Lahore Resolution of the Muslim League.

You must admit that the Resolution itself makes no reference to the two nations theory. In the course of our discussions, you have passionately pleaded that India contains two nations, i.e., Hindus and Muslims, and that the latter have their homelands in India as the former have theirs. The more our argument progresses, the more alarming your picture appears to me. It would be alluring if it was true. But my fear is growing that it is wholly unreal. I find no parallel in history for a body of converts and their descendants claiming to be a nation apart from the parent stock. If India was one nation before the advent of Islam, it must remain one in spite of the change of faith of a very large body of her children.

You do not claim to be a separate nation by right of conquest, but by reason of acceptance of Islam. Will the two nations become one if the whole of India accepted Islam? Will Bengalis, Oriyas, Andhras, Tamilians, Maharashtrians, Gujaratis, etc., cease to have their special characteristics if all of them become converts to Islam? These have all become one politically because they are subject to one foreign control. They are trying today to throw off that subjection.

You seem to have introduced a new test of nationhood. If I accept it, I would have to subscribe to many more claims and face an insoluble problem. The only real, though awful, test of our nationhood arises out of our common political subjection. If you and I throw off this subjection by our combined effort, we shall be born a politically free nation out of our travail. If by then we have not learnt to prize our freedom, we may quarrel among ourselves and, for want of a common master holding us together in his iron grip, seek to split up into small groups or nationalities. There will be nothing to prevent us from descending to that level and we shall not have to go in search of a master. There are many claimants to the throne that never remains vacant.

With this background, I shall present you with my difficulty in accepting your Resolution.

1. Pakistan is not in the Resolution. Does it bear the original meaning Punjab, Afghanistan, Kashmir, Sind and Baluchistan, out of which the name was mnemonically formed? If not what is it?

2. Is the goal of Pakistan pan-Islam?

3. What is it that distinguishes an Indian Muslim from every other Indian, if not his religion? Is he different from a Turk or an Arab?

4. What is the connotation of the word "Muslims" in the Resolution under discussion? Does it mean the Muslims of India of geography or of the Pakistan to be?

5. Is the Resolution addressed to the Muslims by way of education, or to the inhabitants of the whole of India by way of appeal, or to the foreign ruler as an ultimatum?

6. Are the constituents in the two zones to constitute "Independent States", an undefined number in each zone?

7. Is the demarcation to take place during the pendency of British Rule?

8. If the answer to the last question is in the affirmative, the proposal must be accepted first by Britain and then imposed upon India, not evolved from within by the free will of the people of India.

9. Have you examined the position and satisfied yourself that these "Independent States" will be materially and otherwise benefitted by being split up into fragments?

10. Please satisfy me that these Independent Sovereign States will not become a collection of poor States, a menace to themselves and to the rest of India.

11. Pray show me by facts and figures or otherwise how the independence and welfare of India as a whole can be brought about by the acceptance of the Resolution?

12. How are the Muslims under the Princes to be disposed of as a result of this scheme?

13. What is your definition of "minorities"?

14. Will you please define the "adequate, effective and mandatory safeguards" for minorities referred to in the second part of the Resolution?

15. Do you not see that the Lahore Resolution contains only a bare statement of the objective and does not give any idea as to the means to be adopted for the execution of the idea and the concrete corollaries thereof? For instance: (a) Are the people in the regions falling under the plan to have any voice in the matter of separation and, if so, how is it to be ascertained? (b) What is the provision for Defence and similar matters of common concern contemplated in the Lahore Resolution? (c) There are many groups of Muslims who have continuously expressed dissent from the policy of the League. While I am prepared to accept the preponderating influence and position of the League and have approached you for that very reason, is it not our joint duty to remove their

doubts and carry them with us by making them feel that they and their supporters have not been practically disfranchised? (d) Does this not lead again to placing the Resolution of the League before the people of the zones concerned as a whole for acceptance?

As I write this letter and imagine the working of the Resolution in practice, I see nothing but ruin for the whole of India. Believe me, I approach you as a seeker. Though I represent nobody but myself, I aspire to represent all the inhabitants of India, for I realise in my own person their misery and degradation, which is their common lot, irrespective of class, caste or creed. I know that you have acquired a unique hold on the Muslim masses. I want you to use your influence for their total welfare, which must include the rest.

In this hastily written letter, I have only given an inkling of my difficulty.

Yours sincerely,

M. K. GANDHI

September 15, 1944

DEAR QUAID-E-AZAM,

I have yours of the 14th instant, received at 9.40 a.m.

I woke up at 3 a.m. today to finish my promised letter on the Lahore Resolution.

There is no mistake about the date, for I wrote in answer to your reminder of the 13th instant.

Independence does mean as envisaged in the A.I.C.C. Resolution of 1942. But it cannot be on the basis of a united India. If we come to a settlement, it would be on the basis of the settlement, assuming, of course, that it accrues general acceptance in the country. The process will be somewhat like this. We reach by joint effort independence for India as it stands. India becoming free will proceed to demarcation, plebiscite and partition if the people concerned vote for partition. All this is implied in the Rajaji Formula.

As to the provisional interim government, I am afraid I cannot carry my answer any further than I have done. Though I have no scheme for the provisional government, if you have one in connection with the Lahore Resolution, which also, I presume, requires an interim government, we can discuss it.

The Formula was framed by Rajaji in good faith. I accepted it in equal good faith. The hope was that you would look at it with favour. We still think it to be the best in the circumstances. You and I have to put flesh on it, if we can. I have explained the process we have to go through. You have no objection to it. Perhaps, you want to know how I would form the provisional government if I was invited thereto. If I was in that unenviable position, I would see all the claimants and endeavour to satisfy them. My co-operation will be available in that task.

I can give you full satisfaction about your inquiry, "What I would like to know would be, what will be the powers of such a provisional interim government, how it will be formed, to whom it will be responsible." The provisional interim government will be responsible to the elected members of the present Assembly or a newly elected one. It will have all the powers less that of the Commander-in-Chief'during the war and full powers thereafter. It will be the authority to give effect to the agreement that may be arrived at between the League and the Congress and ratified by the other parties.

Yours sincerely,

M. K. GANDHI

September 19, 1944

DEAR QUAID-E-AZAM,

Many thanks for yours of the 17th instant.

124

I am sorry to have to say that your answers omitting 1, 2 and 6 do not give satisfaction.

It may be that all my questions do not arise from the view of mere clarification of the Lahore Resolution. But I contend that they are very relevant from the standpoint of a seeker that I am. You cannot expect anyone to agree to or shoulder the burden of the claim contained in the Lahore Resolution without, for instance, answering my questions 15 (a) and 15 (b) which you brush aside as not arising by way of clarification.

Dr. Ambedkar's thesis, while it is ably written, has carried no conviction to me. The other book mentioned by you, I am sorry to say, I have not seen.

Why can you not accept my statement that I aspire to represent all the sections that compose the people of India? Do you not aspire? Should not every Indian? That the aspiration may never be realised is beside the point.

I am beholden to you, in spite of your opinion about me, for having patience with me. I hope you will never lose it, but will persevere in your effort to convert me. I ask you to take me with my strong views and even prejudices, if I am guilty of any.

As to your verdict on my policy and programme, we must agree to differ. For, I am wholly unrepentant. My purpose is as a lover of communal unity to place my services at your disposal.

I hope you do not expect me to accept the Lahore Resolution without understanding its implications. If your letter is the final word, there is little hope. Can we not agree to differ on the question of "two nations" and yet solve the problem on the basis of self-determination? It is this basis that has brought me to you. If the regions holding Muslim majorities have to be separated according to the Lahore Resolution, the grave step of separation should be specifically placed before and approved by the people in that area.

Yours sincerely,

M. K. GANDHI

DEAR QUAID-E-AZAM,

Your letter of yesterday (21st instant) so disturbed me that I thought I would postpone my reply till after we had met at the usual time. Though I made no advance at our meeting, I think I see some- what clearly what you are driving at. The more I think about the two-nation theory the more alarming it appears to be. The book recommended by you gives me no help. It contains half-truths and its conclusions or inferences are unwarranted. I am unable to accept the proposition that the Muslims of India are a nation, distinct from the rest of the inhabitants of India. Mere assertion is no proof. The consequences of accepting such a proposition are dangerous in the extreme. Once the principle is admitted, there would be no limit to claims for cutting up India into numerous divisions, which would spell India's ruin. I have, therefore, suggested a way out. Let it be a partition as between two brothers, if a division there must be.

You seem to be averse to a plebiscite. In spite of the admitted importance of the League, there must be clear proof that the people affected desire partition. In my opinion, all the people inhabiting the area ought to express their opinion specifically on this single issue of division. Adult suffrage is the best method, but I would accept any other equivalent.

You summarily reject the idea of common interest between the two arms. I can be no willing party to a division which does not provide for the simultaneous safeguarding of common interests, such as Defence, Foreign Affairs and

126

the like. There will be no feeling of security by the people of India without a recognition of the neutural and mutual obligations arising out of physical contiguity.

Your letter shows a wide divergence of opinion and outlook between us. Thus you adhere to the opinion often expressed by you that the August 1942 Resolution is "inimical to the ideals and demands of Muslim India". There is no proof for this sweeping statement.

We seem to be moving in a circle. I have made a suggestion. If we are bent on agreeing, as I hope we are, let us call in a third party or parties to guide or even arbitrate between us.

Yours sincerely,

M. K. GANDHI

September 23, 1944

DEAR QUAID-E-AZAM,

Last evening's talk has left a bad taste in the mouth. Our talks and our correspondence seem to run in parallel lines and never touch one another. We reached the breaking point last evening but, thank God, we were unwilling to part. We resumed discussion and suspended it in order to allow me to keep my time for the evening public prayer.

In order that all possibility of making any mistake in a matter of this great importance may be removed I would like you to give me in writing what precisely on your part you would want me to put my signature to.

I adhere to my suggestion that we may call in some outside assistance to help us at this stage.

Yours sincerely,

M. K. GANDHI

BHAI JINNAH,

I was wondering what I shall send you today. It should be fair on my part to let you and your sister share equally the crisp chapatis they make for me. Here is your share. Please regard it as a token of my love and do please help yourself to it.

Id greetings from

M. K. GANDHI

September 24, 1944

DEAR QUAID-E-AZAM,

I have your two letters of September 23 in reply to my letters of the 22nd and 23rd.

With your assistance, I am exploring the possibilities of reaching an agreement, so that the claim embodied in the Muslim League Resolution of Lahore may be reasonably satisfied. You must, therefore, have no apprehensions that the August Resolution will stand in the way of our reaching an agreement. That Resolution dealt with the question of India as against Britain, and it cannot stand in the way of our settlement.

I proceed on the assumption that India is not to be regarded as two or more nations, but as one family consisting of many members of whom the Muslims living in the north-west zones, i.e., Baluchistan, Sind, North-West Frontier Province and that part of the Punjab where they are in absolute majority over all the other elements and in parts of Bengal and Assam where they are in absolute majority, desire to live in separation from the rest of India.

Differing from you on the general basis, I can yet recommend to the Congress and the country the acceptance of the claim for separation contained in the Muslim League Resolution of Lahore, 1940, on my basis and on the following terms:

The areas should be demarcated by a commission, approved by the Congress and the League. The wishes of the inhabitants of the area demarcated should be ascertained through the votes of the adult population of the areas or through some equivalent method.

If the vote is in favour of separation, it shall be agreed that these areas shall form a separate State as soon as possible after India is free from foreign domination and can, therefore, be constituted into two sovereign independent States.

There shall be a treaty of separation, which should also provide for the efficient and satisfactory administration of Foreign Affairs, Defence, Internal Communications, Customs, Commerce and the like, which must necessarily continue to be matters of common interest between the contracting parties.

The treaty shall also contain terms for safeguarding the rights of minorities in the two States.

Immediately on the acceptance of this agreement by the Congress and the League, the two shall decide upon a common course of action for the attainment of the independence of India.

The League will, however, be free to remain out of any direct action, to which the Congress may resort and in which the League may not be willing to participate.

If you do not agree to these terms, could you let me know in precise terms what you would have me to accept in terms of the Lahore Resolution and bind myself to recommend to the Congress? If you could kindly do this, I shall be able to see, apart from the difference in approach, what definite terms I can agree to. In your letter of 23rd September, you refer to "the basis and fundamental principles embodied in the Lahore Resolution" and ask me to accept them. Surely, this is unnecessary when, as I feel, I have accepted the concrete consequence that should follow from such acceptance.

Yours sincerely,

M. K. GANDHI

September 25, 1944

DEAR QUAID-E-AZAM,

Yesterday's talk leads me to inflict this letter on you, which I trust you will not mind.

Our conversations have come about as a result of your correspondence with Rajaji in July last over his Formula and your consultations with the League Working Committee thereon, and my own letter to you suggesting a meeting between you and me. My proposal of yesterday is an earnest effort to meet the essential requirements of the Lahore Resolution. I would like you, therefore, to think fifty times before throwing away an offer which had been made entirely in the spirit of service in the cause of communal harmony. Do not take, I pray, the responsibility of rejecting the offer. Throw it on your Council. Give me an opportunity of addressing them. If they feel like rejecting it, I would like you to advise the Council to put it before the open session of the League. If you will accept my advice and permit me, I would attend the open session and address it.

You are too technical when you dismiss my proposal for arbitration or outside guidance over points of difference. If I have approached you as an individual, and not in any representative capacity, it is because we believe that if I reach an agreement with you, it will be of material use in the process of securing a Congress-League settlement and acceptance of it by the country. Is it irrelevant or inadmissible to supplement our efforts to convince each other without help, guidance, advice or even arbitration?

Yours sincerely,

M. K. GANDHI

September 26, 1944

DEAR QUAID-E-AZAM,

In view of my letter to you of yesterday, left to myself, I would have refrained from dealing with your letter before our meeting today. But I have deferred to Rajaji's advice to finish the chain of correspondence.

I confess I am unable to understand your persistent refusal to appreciate the fact that the Formula presented to you by me in my letter of the 24th as well as the Formula presented to you by Rajaji give you virtually what is embodied in the Lahore Resolution, providing at the same time what is absolutely necessary to make the arrangement acceptable to the country. You keep on saying that I should accept certain theses, while I have been contending that the best way for us, who differ in our approach to the problem, is to give body to the demand as it stands in the Resolution and work it out to our mutual satisfaction. It is on this plan that I understand Rajaji's Formula is to be conceived, and it is on the same plan that I have tried to work it out in the course of and as a result of our talks. I contend that either gives you the substance of the Lahore Resolution. Unfortunately, you reject both. And I cannot accept the Lahore Resolution as you want me to, especially when you seek to introduce into its interpretation theories and claims which I cannot accept and which I cannot ever hope to induce India to accept.

Your constant references to my not being clothed with representative authority are really irrelevant. I have approached you so that, if you and I can agree upon a common course of action, I may use what influence I possess for its acceptance by the Congress and the country. If you break, it cannot be because I have no representative capacity, or because I have been unwilling to give you satisfaction in regard to the claim embodied in the Lahore Resolution.

Yours sincerely,
M. K. GANDHI

131

NEW DELHI,
June 14, 1947

DEAR QAID-E-AZAM,

Yours of the 13th instant was received when I was at a meeting.

I had hoped that H. E. had not clearly understood your meaning. I now see that I was mistaken. I cannot ask the Congress to commit hara-kiri.

Yours sincerely,

M. K. GANDHI

[October 11, 1947]

MY DEAR QAID-E-AZAM,

Shaheed Saheb has reported to me your reactions to my endorsement on the suggestions drafted by him. I am sorry to learn about it. I would never intend to give my casual remark the sinister meaning you are reported to have given it. In any case Shaheed Saheb's suggestions I endorse subject as follows:

In paragraph 2(4) of his letter to you—I would add:"and will submit to a tribunal of permanent arbitration selected from Indians alone (i.e., from the members of the two Dominions)." In Paragraph 2(8) or in any other suitable place, I would like the following idea to be brought out: "Each State will induce the refugees to return and occupy their respective homes."

I find that this idea to some extent is brought out in paragraph 3 of the declaration. It should be emphasised and steps taken to implement it.

In my opinion, some such agreement as suggested by Shaheed Saheb should precede any move for hearty co-operation between the two States. What is wanted no doubt is like mind, like word and like action between the two.

□

# Letters to Lord Mountbatten

Lord Mountbatten took over as Viceroy and Governor-General of India on the 24th March, 1947. Perhaps, he wanted to meet Gandhi on that day, so he wrote him a letter, two days earlier, on the 22nd March which conveyed his wish to meet him. At that time, Gandhiji was busy in pacifying the disturbances in Bihar, which was his third and last visit to Bihar. He wrote him back that he would visit him only after the 28th of that month.

Immediately after laking over as Viceroy and Governor-General, Lord Mountbatten, in place of pacifying and establishing Hindu-Muslim Unity, worked to ignite and speed up the partition. He not only divided India but also freed all the small 'Riyasats', all over the country in order to further weaken it. (562 of them merged with India alone.)

Lord Mountbatten was Louis Mountbatten, the 1st Earl. His original name was Louis Francis Albert Victor Nicholas. He was the Prince of Battenberg. He was born on the 25 June, 1900 at Frogmore house, Windsor, England. He was killed on the 27th August, 1979 in Bonegal Bay, off Mulaghmore, County Sligo while on a sailing visit to Ireland. He was actually assassinated by Irish terrorists who planted a bomb on his boat.

Lord Mountbatten was a British statesman and Naval Commander. He was the son of Prince Louis of Battenberg. He was the great-grandson of Queen Victoria. He entered the Royal Navy in 1913 and became an aide to the Prince of Wales in 1921.

In the World War II, he was allied commander for Southeast Asia from 1943 to 46. He directed the capture of Burma, so he is also known as Mountbatten of Burma.

In 1947, he was appointed the Viceroy of India. As viceroy, he administered the transfer of power from Britain to divided but the independent nations of India and Pakistan. He served as the Governor-General of India during 1947 and 48 when C. Raja Gopalachari took over from him. Later on, he became the first sea lord from 1955 to 59, and Chief of the United Kingdom Defence Staff from 1959 to 65.

Gandhiji sent him a nice 'Khādi Table Cloth', as wedding gift. Lord and Lady Mountbatten personally delivered the gift to Princess Elizabeth. It was prominently exhibited among the wedding gifts at St. James. On his return, he conveyed to Gandhiji a personal message of appreciation and thanks from the Princess and the Prince consort. They were touched by that very fine gesture of Gandhiji.

ॐ

PATNA,
March 26, 1947

DEAR FRIEND,

I thank you for your letter of the 22nd instant received by me yesterday.

You have rightly gauged my difficulty about moving out of Bihar at the present moment. But I dare not resist your kind call. I am just now leaving for one of the disturbed areas of Bihar. Will you therefore forgive me if I do not send you the exact date of my departure for Delhi? I return from this third Bihar tour on the 28th instant. My departure will therefore be as quickly as I can arrange it after the 28th.

In order that this may be in your hands as early as possible I send this through His Excellency the Governor of Bihar.

Yours sincerely,

M. K. GANDHI

H. E. LORD LOUIS MOUNTBATTEN OF BURMA,
NEW DELHI
[PS.]

*I expect to leave for New Delhi on the 30th instant.*

❀ ❀ ❀

1 AURANGZEB ROAD, NEW DELHI,
April 8, 1947

DEAR FRIEND,

Many thanks for your two letters of the 7th inst.

As to the first, I am glad that as I read it, whatever misunderstanding, if there was any, was of no consequence.

As to the second letter, the weather would not stand in the way of my going to the Punjab. I must ask the voice within for the final guidance. If I do go, I shall let you know the date.

Of course, you can rely upon my help no matter wherever I happen to be at the time.

Yours sincerely,

M. K. GANDHI

❀ ❀ ❀

BIRLA HOUSE,
NEW DELHI,
November 9, 1947

DEAR LORD MOUNTBATTEN,

This little thing is made out of doubled yarn of my own spinning. The knitting was done by a Punjabi girl who was trained by Abha's husband, my grandson. Lady Mountbatten knows Abha. Please give the bride and the bridegroom this with my blessings, with the wish that they would have a long and happy life of service of men.

I hope you will have a happy time and safe return according to your time-table.

Yours sincerely,

M. K. GANDHI

❀    ❀    ❀

BHANGI COLONY,
READING ROAD, NEW DELHI
Personal and Immediate
April 7, 1947

DEAR FRIEND,

I have pressing letters from friends in the Punjab asking me to go there even if it be for a few days. Pandit Nehru agrees. Nevertheless I would like you to guide me too.

Then Noakhali calls. If wires received by me during the last two days are to be relied upon, there is increasing lawlessness in Noakhali. Attempts at roasting people alive have been traced twice, and loot, etc., is going on. You will see my public statement in the press.

This outbreak of violence is not a mere detail. If it cannot be dealt with now, it won't be fourteen months hence.

Yours sincerely,

M. K. GANDHII

HIS EXCELLENCY THE VICEROY
NEW DELHI

❀    ❀    ❀

June 2, 1947

I am sorry I can't speak; when I took the decision about the Monday silence I did reserve two exceptions, i.e., about speaking to high functionaries on urgent matters or attending upon sick people. But I know you do not want me to break my silence.

Have I said one word against you during my speeches? If you admit that I have not, your warning is superfluous.

There are one or two things I must talk about, but not today. If we meet each other again I shall speak.

Badshah Khan is with me in the Bhangi Colony. He said "Do ask the Viceroy to remove the Governor. We won't have peace till he is gone." I don't know whether he is right or wrong. He is truthful. If it can be done decorously, you should do it.

NEW DELHI,
June 10/11, 1947

DEAR FRIEND,

The Rajkumari has given me the purport of you conversation with her.

Though you have been good enough to tell me that I could see you at any time I wanted to, I must not avail myself of the kindness. I would like, however, to reduce to writing some of the things I hold to be necessary for the proper and swift working of the scheme.

1.  As to the referendum in the Frontier Province I must confess that my idea does not commend itself to Pandit Nehru and his colleagues. As I told you, if my proposal did not commend itself to them, I would not have the heart to go any further with it.

2.  This, however, does not in any way affect my proposal that before proceeding with the referendum, you should invite Qaid-e- Azam Jinnah to proceed to the Frontier Province and to woo the Ministers including Badshah Khan and his Khudai Khidmatgars who have made the province what it is—better or worse. Before he goes, no doubt, he should be assured of a courteous hearing from them.

137

3. Whether he favours the idea or not, Qaid-e-Azam should be asked to give a fair picture of the Pakistan scheme before the simple Pathan mind is asked to make its choice of Hindustan or Pakistan. I fancy that the Pathan knows his position in Hindustan. If he does not, the Congress or the Constituent Assembly now at work should be called upon to complete the picture. It will be unfair, I apprehend, to choose between Hindustan or Pakistan without knowing what each is. He should at least know where his entity will be fully protected.

4. There is as yet no peace in the Frontier Province. Can there be a true referendum when strife has not completely abated? Minds are too heated to think coherently. Neither the Congress nor the League can disown liability for disturbances by their followers. If peace does not reign in the land, the whole superstructure will come to pieces and you will, in spite of division, leave behind a legacy of which you will not be proud.

5. The sooner you have a homogeneous ministry the better. In no case can the League nominees work independently of the whole Cabinet. It is a vicious thing that there is no joint responsibility for every act of individual members.

6. The only way to keep the wonderful time-table made by you is to anticipate the future and ask your special staff to work out all the items presented by you, without reference to the Cabinet and then when the time comes, the report should be presented to the respective parties for acceptance, amendment or rejection.

7. The more I see things the more firmly I believe that the States' problem presents a variety of difficulties which demand very serious and fearless treatment on your part.

8. The problem of the civil and military services, though in a way not equally difficult, demands the same firm handling as the States. Gurgaon strife is an instance in

point. So far as I know one single officer is responsible for the continuance of the mischief.

9. Lastly may I suggest that the attempt to please all parties is a fruitless and thankless task. In the course of our conver-sation I suggested that equal praise bestowed on both the parties was not meant. No praise would have been the right thing. 'Duty will be merit when debt becomes a donation.' It is not too late to mend. Your undoubted skill as a warrior was never more in demand than today. Fancy a sailor without his fleet, save his mother wit!

10. I have tried to be as succinct as possible. I could not be briefer. If any of the points raised herein demand a personal talk, you have but to appoint the suitable time. Please do not think of calling me for the sake of courtesy.

11. I received you kind note of 10th instant whilst I had almost finished this note. It does not call for a separate reply.

This was finished at 9.25 p.m. It will be typed tomorrow.

Yours sincerely,

M. K. GANDHI

H. E. THE VICEROY
NEW DELHI

NEW DELHI,
June 13, 1947

DEAR FRIEND,

Your two letters of 12th instant were received last night for which I thank you. I have sent a letter to Qaid-e-Azam Jinnah of which a copy is enclosed herewith. The condition precedent to the Qaid-e-Azam accepting my suggestion is dangerous in its implication. My suggestion is simply what I conveyed to you in my letter of 11th instant.

Before proceeding with the referendum you should invite Qaide- Azam Jinnah to proceed to the Frontier Province to woo the Ministers including Badshah Khan and the Khudai Khidmatgars. . . I have added, "Before he goes, no doubt, he should be assured a courteous hearing from them." The visit, therefore, if it takes place, will take place for convincing and converting the Ministers and Badshah Khan and his Khudai Khidmatgars. It should in no sense be a propaganda tour. I hope both you and Her Excellency would have a quiet and cool weekend in Simla.

Yours sincerely,

M. K. GANDHI

H.E. THE VICEROY

NEW DELHI,
June 27, 1947

DEAR FRIEND,

Panditji was with me at noon and I gave him the purport of the conversation about Kashmir and he immediately asked whether the lettter you were kindly sending to the Maharaja Saheb was going by wire or post. I could not give him a satisfactory answer and I said it would probably be by post. He said the letter would take some days to reach there and the reply too might be delayed. I share his anxiety that the matter brooks no delay. For him it is one of personal honour. I have simply undertaken to replace him to the best of my ability. I would like to free him from anxiety in this matter. I seek your aid.

Yours sincerely,

M. K. GANDHI

H. E. THE VICEROY
NEW DELHI

DEAR FRIEND,

I sent you a note in the afternoon. The time after the evening prayer and walk I wish to devote to talking to you on certain matters I was able to touch but could not develop when we met.

I told the Parliamentary Delegation that heralded the Cabinet Mission and the Cabinet Mission itself that they had to choose between the two parties or even three. They were doomed to fail if they tried to please all, holding them all to be in the right. I had hoped that you were bravely and honestly trying to extricate yourself from the impossible position. But my eyes were opened when, if I understood you correctly, you said that Qaid-e-Azam Jinnah and the League members were equally in the right with the Congress members and that possibly Qaid-e-Azam Jinnah was more so. I suggested that this is not humanly possible. One must be wholly right in the comparative sense. You have to make your choice at this very critical stage in the history of this country. If you think that Qaid-e-Azam Jinnah is, on the whole, more correct and more reasonable than the Congress, you should choose the League as your advisers and in all matters be frankly and openly guided by them.

You threw out a hint that Qaid-e-Azam might not be able to let you quit even by 15th August especially if the Congress members did not adopt a helpful attitude. This was for me a startling statement. I pointed the initial mistake of the British being party to splitting India into two. It is not possible to undo the mistake. But I hold that it is quite possible and necessary not to put a premium upon the mistake. This does not in any way impinge upon the very admirable doctrine of fair play. Fair play demands that I do not help the mistaken party to fancy that the mistake was no mistake but a belated and only a partial discharge of an obligation.

141

You startled me again by telling me that, if the partition had not been made during British occupation, the Hindus being the major party would have never allowed partition and held the Muslims by force under subjection. I told you that this was a grave mistake. The question of numbers was wholly untenable in this connection. I cited the classic example of less than one hundred thousand British soldiers holding India under utter subjection. You saw no analogy between the two instances. I suggested the difference was only one of degree.

I place the following for your consideration:

(a) The Congress has solemnly declared that it would not hold by force any Province within the Union.

(b) It is physically impossible for millions of caste-ridden Hindus to hold well-knit though fewer millions of Muslims under subjection by force.

(c) It must not be forgotten that Muslim dynasties have progressively subjugated India by exactly the same means as the English conquerors later did.

(d) Already there has been a movement to win over to the Muslim side the so-called scheduled classes and the so-called aboriginal races.

(e) The caste Hindus who are the bugbear are, it can be shown conclusively, a hopeless minority. Of these the armed Rajputs are not yet nationalists as a class. The Brahmins and the Banias are still untrained in the use of arms. Their supremacy where it exists is purely moral. The Sudras count, I am sorry, more as scheduled class than anything else. That such Hindu society by reason of its mere superiority in numbers can crush millions of Muslims is an astounding myth.

This should show you why, even if I am alone, I swear by nonviolence and truth together standing for the highest order of courage before which the atom bomb pales into insignificance, what to say of a fleet of Dreadnoughts.

I have not shown this to any of my friends.

If I have misunderstood you in any single particular you have only to correct me and I shall gladly accept the correction. If I am obscure anywhere, I shall try to remove the obscurity either by letter or by meeting according to your wish.

My anxiety to save you from mistakes as I see them is the sole excuse for this letter.

Yours sincerely,

M. K. GANDHI

H. E. THE VICEROY

NEW DELHI

BHANGI COLONY,
NEW DELHI,
July 5, 1947

DEAR FRIEND,

I thank you for your letter which came into my hands after the evening prayer.

Agitation is undoubtedly being carried on today by Badshah Khan and his lieutenants to tell the voters that it is wrong for them to take part in the voting. There should be no demonstration during the voting days and there should be no approach to the voters during the voting time. If this is what you mean I shall be glad to refer to the matter in those terms at the evening prayer. I am quite prepared to adopt quicker means of reaching Badshah Khan, if you suggest any.

If you have any other thing in view, you will please let me know.

Yours sincerely,

M. K. GANDHI

H. E. THE VICEROY

NEW DELHI

NEW DELHI,
July 5, 1947

DEAR FRIEND,

I received your kind letter of even date just after I had finished my prayer speech and was going out for my walk. Fortunately about noon I had a visit from a Pathan whom I had known to be a Khudai Khidmatgar. He was going to Peshawar and so I gave him the message which I have reproduced in the letter I enclose herewith. You may read the letter and if you think that it covers the new point you have raised you may send the letter by special messenger as suggested by you. I am hoping that there will be no disturbance on the part of Badshah Khan and his followers. In the message that I sent through the Pathan Khudai Khidmatgar I covered much more ground than mentioned in me letter to Badshah Khan.

I thank you for giving me the purport of the telegram received by you from the Resident in Kashmir.

I hope Her Excellency was none the worse for her visit to the Bhangi Basti.

It is open to you not to send the enclosed if it does not merit your approval.

Yours sincerely,

M. K. GANDHI

H. E. THE VICEROY
NEW DELHI

BHANGI COLONY,
NEW DELHI,
July 11, 1947

DEAR FRIEND,

I am still without any news from Kashmir. I wonder if you can remind the Maharaja. If I was not bound by any promise made to you, of course I would not want any permission to

144

go to Kashmir. I would simply go as any private person.

Yours sincerely,

M. K. GANDHI
H. E. THE VICEROY
NEW DELHI

BHANGI COLONY,
NEW DELHI,
July 16, 1947

DEAR FRIEND,

I had a long talk with Panditji about Kashmir. He is firmly of opinion that I should go in any case, not minding if Qaid-e-Azam Jinnah or his deputy goes after my visit. He thinks, and I agree, that if now my visit is postponed, it will disappoint many persons in Kashmir. That I may not be allowed to see Sheikh Abdulla Saheb should not affect the contemplated visit one way or the other. In the circumstances, I suggest that you should telegraph to the Maharaja Saheb that as my visit would not mean any speeches or public meetings, it should not cause any embarrassment to the State and that I should go to Kashmir at the earliest possible moment.

As I have said to you my suggestion is subject to your wish not to interfere with Panditji's wishes in the matter. If, for any reason, you wish otherwise, I would not go.

If I go, I would go as a private visitor. Hence I would not think of putting the Maharaja Saheb to any trouble on my account. Friends would make arrangements for my stay.

Finally, I should add that if, for any reason, I do not go to Kashmir, most probably Panditji would want to go for two or three days though he would prefer my going.

Yours sincerely,

M. K. GANDHI
H. E. THE VICEROY
NEW DELHI

NEW DELHI,
July 28, 1947

DEAR FRIEND,

It is my silence day. Hence this infliction in the shape of my handwriting.

Pandit Nehru told me last night that as there were hitches about my going to Kashmir, he had decided to go even if only for two or three days. Thus I am now free to go to Bihar and thence to Noakhali. Before doing so, I might go for two days to the Punjab. I should like to leave Delhi tomorrow. You wanted me to see you before leaving. If the need is still felt, I am at your disposal tomorrow. You will then name the hour.

May I say I deeply appreciated your wish to go to an unpretentious house as the chosen Governor-General of the millions of the half-famished villagers of the nation. I hope it will be possible to carry out the wish.

Yours sincerely,

M. K. GANDHI

H. E. THE VICEROY

CALCUTTA,
August 30, 1947

DEAR FRIEND,

Many thanks for your letter which His Excellency the Governor sent me yesterday afternoon. I do not know if Shaheed Saheb and I can legitimately appropriate the compliment you pay us. Probably suitable conditions were ready for us to take the credit for what appears to have been a magical performance.

Am I right in gathering from your letter that you would like me to try the same thing for the Punjab? I am in correspondence with the Pandit and the Sardar.

I hope your new office is not unduly more arduous than as Viceroy.

It filled me with joy when I read in the papers that Lady Mountbatten had flown to the Punjab. I hope she is none the worse for the trying visit.

Yours sincerely,

M. K. GANDHI

H. E. THE LORD MOUNTBATTEN OF BURMA
GOVERNMENT HOUSE
NEW DELHI

NEW DELHI,
October 23, 1947

DEAR FRIEND,

I have spoken to Pandit Nehru. But he is adamant. He is firmly of opinion that no change should be made until the weather has cleared. If it does, it may take two or three months. In this estimate I agree with him.

Yours sincerely

M. K. GANDHI

H. E. LORD MOUNTBATTEN OF BURMA
GOVERNMENT HOUSE
NEW DELHI

□

# Letters to Lord Wavell

It was Lord Warell, the then Viceroy of India, who continued the effort to form an Indian Government, which the Cabinet Mission had initiated; even when the Mission had left Delhi. He readily announced the formation of an Interim National Government headed by the Viceroy as the President. It replaced the Viceroy's Excutive Council. The Congress President, J.L. Nehru was to be its Vice-President. The Muslim League refused to join the Government on the pretext that they were not given an exclusive right to nominate the Muslim Members in the Cabinet. The Interim Government took office without Muslim League on the 2nd September 1946.

Archibald Percival Wavell, popularly known as Lord Wavell, was born on 5th May 1883 in England at Colchester, Essex. He died in London on the 24th May, 1950. He was famous as an excellent trainer to troops. In 1939, he was appointed the British Commander in Chief for the Middle East. During the World War II he became famous, as he defeated numerically a very superior Italian Army in African Campaign during 1940 and 41. During 1941-43, as the commander in Chief of Southeast Asia, he was noted for his defeat at the hands of Japanese who won Malaya, Singapore and Burma. Later on, he became the Field Marshal. He served as the Viceroy of India during 1943 to 47.

৪৩০৪

DEAR FRIEND,

Although I have not had the pleasure of meeting you, I address you on purpose as "dear friend". I am looked upon by the representatives of the British Government as a great, if not the greatest, enemy of the British. Since I regard myself as a friend and servant of humanity including the British, in token of my goodwill I call you, the foremost representative of the British in India, my "friend".

2. I have received in common with some others, a notice informing me, for the first time, why I am detained and conferring on me the right of representation against my detention. I have duly sent my reply, but I have as yet heard nothing from the Government. A reminder, too, has gone after a wait of thirteen days.

3. I have said some only have received notices because out of the six of us in this camp, only three have received them. I presume that all will receive them in due course. But my mind is filled with the suspicion that the notices have been sent as a matter of form only, and not with any intention to do justice. I do not wish to burden this letter with argument. I repeat what I said in the correspondence with your predecessor, that the Congress and I are wholly innocent of the charges brought against us. Nothing but an impartial tribunal to investigate the Government case, and the Congress case against the Government, will bring out the truth.

4. The speeches recently made on behalf of the Government in the Assembly on the release motion, and on the gagging order on Shri Sarojini Devi, I consider to be playing with fire. I distinguish between defeat of Japanese arms and Allied victory. The latter must carry with it the deliverance of India from the foreign yoke. The spirit of India demands complete freedom from all foreign dominance and would, therefore, resist

Japanese yoke equally with British or any other. The Congress represents that spirit in full measure. It has grown to be an institution whose roots have gone deep down into the Indian soil. I was, therefore, staggered to read that Government were satisfied with things as they were going. Had they not got from among the Indian people the men and money they wanted? Was not the Government machinery running smooth? This self satisfaction bodes ill for Britain, India and the world, if it does not quickly give place to a searching of hearts in British high places.

5. Promises for the future are valueless in the face of the world struggle in which the fortune of all nations and therefore of the whole of humanity is involved. Present performance is the peremptory need of the moment, if the war is to end in world peace and not be a preparation for another war bloodier than the present, if indeed there can be a bloodier. Therefore, real war effort must mean satisfaction of India's demand. "Quit India" only gives vivid expression to that demand and has not the sinister and poisonous meaning attributed to it without warrant by the Government of India. The expression is charged with the friendliest feeling for Britain in terms of the whole of humanity.

6. I have done. I thought that, if I claim to be a friend of the British, as I do, nothing should deter me from sharing my deepest thoughts with you. It is no pleasure for me to be in this camp, where all my creature comforts are supplied without any effort on my part, when I know that millions outside are starving for want of food. But I should feel utterly helpless, if I went out and missed the food by which alone living becomes worth while.

I am,

Yours sincerely,
M. K. GANDHI

❀ ❀ ❀

'MANOR VILLE,'
SIMLA WEST,
June 28, 1945

DEAR FRIEND,

Some hangings—an aftermath of the disturbances of 1942— are impending. I have some cases given to me by Dr. Rajendra Prasad of the Working Committee. The Chimur cases you perhaps know. I do not quite know how the last stages of the conference are shaping. Be that as it may, I suggest that all such hangings be commuted to life sentences without further public appeal or agitation and whether judicial proceedings are going on or not. If you think that this is beyond you, may I suggest that these be postponed so as to be dealt with by the national government that is coming into being?

Yours very sincerely,

M. K. GANDHI

H. E. THE VICEROY
SIMLA

VALMIKI MANDIR,
READING ROAD,
NEW DELHI,
August 28, 1946

DEAR FRIEND,

I write this as a friend and after deep thought.

Several times last evening you repeated that you were a "plain man and a soldier" and that you did not know the law. We are all plain men though we may not all be soldiers and even though some of us may know the law. It is our purpose, I take it, to devise methods to prevent a repetition of the recent terrible happenings in Calcutta. The question before us is how best to do it.

Your language last evening was minatory. As representative of the King you cannot afford to be a military man only, nor

151

to ignore the law, much less the law of your own making. You should be assisted, if necessary, by a legal mind enjoying your full confidence. You threatened not to convene the Constituent Assembly if the formula you placed before Pandit Nehru and me was not acted upon by the Congress. If such be really the case then you should not have made the announcement you did on 12th August. But having made it you should recall the action and form another ministry enjoying your full confidence. If British arms are kept here for internal peace and order, your Interim Government would be reduced to a farce. The Congress cannot afford to impose its will on warring elements in India through the use of British arms. Nor can the Congress be expected to bend itself and adopt what it considers a wrong course because of the brutal exhibition recently witnessed in Bengal. Such submission would itself lead to an encouragement and repetition of such tragedies. The vindictive spirit on either side would go deeper, biding for an opportunity to exhibit itself more fiercely and more disgracefully when occasion occurs. And all this will be chiefly due to the continued presence in India of a foreign power strong in and proud of its arms.

I say this neither as a Hindu nor as a Muslim. I write only as an Indian. In so far as I am aware, the Congress claims to know both the Hindu and Muslim mind more than you or any Britisher can do. Unless, therefore, you can wholly trust the Congress Government which you have announced, you should reconsider your decision, as I have already suggested.

You will please convey the whole of this letter to the British Cabinet.

I am,

Yours sincerely,

M. K. GANDHI

H. E. THE VICEROY
THE VICEROY'S HOUSE
NEW DELHI

□

# A Letter to Lord Irwin

It was the natural outcome of the intense movements that Lord Irwin was forced to reach an understanding with Mahatma Gandhi.

In March 1931, there was a truce-meeting. The government was represented by Lord Edward Irwin. He had decided to negotiate some matters with Gandhi. A pact was signed and it is known as **"Gandhi Irwin Pact"**.

The British Government agreed to free all political prisoners, in return for the suspension of the civil disobedience movement.

As a result of the pact, Gandhi was invited to attend the Round Table Conference in London as the sole representative of Indian National Congress. Gandhi and the nation was disappointed because it focused on the Indian Princess and Indian Minorities, rather than the transfer of power.

৪০৫

SATYAGRHA ASHRAM,
SABARMATI,
March 2, 1930

DEAR FRIEND,

Before embarking on civil disobedience and taking the risk I have dreaded to take all these years, I would fain approach you and find a way out.

153

My personal faith is absolutely clear. I cannot intentionally hurt anything that lives, much less fellow human beings, even though they may do the greatest wrong to me and mine. Whilst, therefore, I hold the British rule to be a curse, I do not intend harm to a single Englishman or to any legitimate interest he may have in India.

I must not be misunderstood. Though I hold the British rule in India to be a curse, I do not, therefore, consider Englishmen in general to be worse than any other people on earth I have the privilege of claiming many Englishmen as dearest friends. Indeed much that I have learnt of the evil of British rule is due to the writings of frank and courageous Englishmen who have not hesitated to tell the unpalatable truth about that rule.

And why do I regard the British rule as a curse?

It has impoverished the dumb millions by a system of progressive exploitation and by a ruinously expensive military and civil administration which the country can never afford.

It has reduced us politically to serfdom. It has sapped the foundations of our culture. And, by the policy of cruel disarmament, it has degraded us spiritually. Lacking the inward strength, we have been reduced, by all but universal disarmament, to a state bordering on cowardly helplessness.

In common with many of my countrymen, I had hugged the fond hope that the proposed Round Table Conference might furnish a solution. But, when you said plainly that you could not give any assurance that you or the British Cabinet would pledge yourselves to support a scheme of full Dominion Status, the Round Table Conference could not possibly furnish the solution for which vocal India is consciously, and the dumb millions are unconsciously, thirsting. Needless to say there never was any question of Parliament's verdict being anticipated. Instances are not wanting of the British Cabinet, in anticipation of the Parliamentary verdict, having pledged itself to a particular policy.

The Delhi interview having miscarried, there was no option for Pandit Motilal Nehru and me but to take steps to carry out the solemn resolution of the Congress arrived at in Calcutta at its Session in 1928.

But the Resolution of Independence should cause no alarm, if the word Dominion Status mentioned in your announcement had been used in its accepted sense. For, has it not been admitted by responsible British statesmen that Dominion Status is virtual Independence? What, however, I fear is that there never has been any intention of granting such Dominion Status to India in the immediate future.

But this is all past history. Since the announcement many events have happened which show unmistakably the trend of British policy.

It seems as clear as daylight that responsible British statesmen do not contemplate any alteration in British policy that might adversely affect Britain's commerce with India or require an impartial and close scrutiny of Britain's transactions with India. If nothing is done to end the process of exploitation India must be bled with an ever increasing speed. The Finance Member regards as a settled fact the 1/6 ratio which by a stroke of the pen drains India of a few crores. And when a serious attempt is being made through a civil form of direct action, to unsettle this fact, among many others, even you cannot help appealing to the wealthy landed classes to help you to crush that attempt in the name of an order that grinds India to atoms.

Unless those who work in the name of the nation understand and keep before all concerned the motive that lies behind the craving for independence, there is every danger of independence coming to us so changed as to be of no value to those toiling voiceless millions for whom it is sought and for whom it is worth taking. It is for that reason that I have been recently telling the public what independence should really mean.

Let me put before you some of the salient points.

The terrific pressure of land revenue, which furnishes a large part of the total, must undergo considerable modification in an independent India. Even the much vaunted permanent settlement benefits the few rich zamindars, not the ryots. The ryot has remained as helpless as ever. He is a mere tenant at will. Not only, then, has the land revenue to be considerably reduced, but the whole revenue system has to be so revised as to make the ryot's good its primary concern. But the British system seems to be designed to crush the very life out of him. Even the salt he must use to live is so taxed as to make the burden fall heaviest on him, if only because of the heartless impartiality of its incidence. The tax shows itself still more burdensome on the poor man when it is remembered that salt is the one thing he must eat more than the rich man both individually and collectively. The drink and drug revenue, too, is derived from the poor. It saps the foundations both of their health and morals. It is defended under the false plea of individual freedom, but, in reality, is maintained for its own sake. The ingenuity of the authors of the reforms of 1919 transferred this revenue to the so-called responsible part of dyarchy, so as to throw the burden of prohibition on it, thus, from the very beginning, rendering it powerless for good. If the unhappy minister wipes out this revenue he must starve education, since in the existing circumstances he has no new source of replacing that revenue. If the weight of taxation has crushed the poor from above, the destruction of the central supplementary industry, i.e., hand-spinning, has undermined their capacity for producing wealth. The tale of India's ruination is not complete without reference to the liabilities incurred in her name. Sufficient has been recently said about these in the public Press. It must be the duty of a free India to subject all the liabilities to the strictest investigation, and repudiate those that may be adjudged by an impartial tribunal to be unjust and unfair.

The iniquities sampled above are maintained in order to carry on a foreign administration, demonstrably the most expensive in the world. Take your own salary. It is over Rs. 21,000 per month, besides many other indirect additions. The British Prime Minister gets £ 5,000 per year, i.e., over Rs. 5,400 per month at the present rate of exchange. You are getting over Rs. 700 per day against India's average income of less than annas 2 per day. The Prime Minister gets Rs. 180 per day against Great Britain's average income of nearly Rs. 2 per day. Thus, you are getting much over five thousand times India's average income. The British Prime Minister is getting only ninety times Britain's average income. On bended knees I ask you to ponder over this phenomenon. I have taken a personal illustration to drive home a painful truth. I have too great a regard for you as a man to wish to hurt your feelings. I know that you do not need the salary you get. Probably the whole of your salary goes for charity. But a system that provides for such an arrangement deserves to be summarily scrapped. What is true of the Viceregal salary is true generally of the whole administration.

A radical cutting down of the revenue, therefore, depends upon an equally radical reduction in the expenses of the administration. This means a transformation of the scheme of government. This transformation is impossible without independence. Hence, in my opinion, the spontaneous demonstration of 26th January, in which hundreds of thousands of villagers instinctively participated. To them independence means deliverance from the killing weight.

Not one of the great British political parties, it seems to me, is prepared to give up the Indian spoils to which Great Britain helps herself from day to day, often, in spite of the unanimous opposition of Indian opinion.

Nevertheless, if India is to live as a nation, if the slow death by starvation of her people is to stop, some remedy must be found for immediate relief. The proposed Conference is certainly not the remedy. It is not a matter of carrying conviction by me the favour not to deflect me from my course unless you can see your way to conform to the substance of this letter.

This letter is not in any way intended as a threat but is a simple and sacred duty peremptory on a civil resister. Therefore, I am having it specially delivered by a young English friend who believes in the Indian cause and is a full believer in non-violence and whom Providence seems to have sent to me, as it were, for the very purpose.

I remain,

Your sincere friend,

M. K. GANDHI

H. E. LORD IRWIN
VICEROY'S HOUSE
NEW DELHI-3

□

# A Letter to the Viceroy

1 DARYAGANJ,
DELHI,
March 23, 1931

DEAR FRIEND,

It seems cruel to inflict this letter on you, but the interest of peace demands a final appeal. Though you were frank enough to tell me that there was little hope of your commuting the sentence of death on Bhagat Singh and two others, you said you would consider my submission of Saturday. Dr. Sapru met me yesterday and said that you were troubled over the matter and taxing your brain as to the proper course to adopt. If there is any room left for reconsideration, I invite your attention to the following.

Popular opinion rightly or wrongly demands commutation. When there is no principle at stake, it is often a duty to respect it.

In the present case the chances are that, if commutation is granted, internal peace is most likely to be promoted. In the event of execution, peace is undoubtedly in danger.

Seeing that I am able to inform you that the revolutionary party has assured me that, in the event of these lives being spared, that party will stay its hands, suspension of sentence pending cessation of revolutionary murders becomes in my opinion a peremptory duty.

Political murders have been condoned before now. It is worth while saving these lives, if thereby many other innocent lives are likely to be saved and maybe even revolutionary crime almost stamped out.

Since you seem to value my influence such as it is in favour of peace, do not please unnecessarily make my position, difficult as it is, almost too difficult for future work.

Execution is an irretrievable act. If you think there is the slightest chance of error of judgment, I would urge you to suspend for further review an act that is beyond recall.

If my presence is necessary, I can come. Though I may not speak, I may hear and write what I want to say.

"Charity never faileth."

I am,

Your sincere friend,

□

# Letters to Mira Behn

Although Mira Behn was an English woman, she was an Indian freedom fighter. Her original name was Madeleine Slade, which is known to very few people. Even people have forgotten that she was an English lady. She was so devoted and dedicated that Gandhi gave her this name 'Mira Behn' and he addressed her that way.

Mira Behn is known as 'the Indian Lady', and the Mira Bai of the 20th century. No one asked or encouraged her to change her religion but without changing the religion she became a true Hindu. She led a simple life, wore coarse Khādi and was proficient in carding and spinning. She lived like a daughter of Gandhi and worked as a bridge between the British Government and Mahatma Gandhi.

Mira Behn was born on 22 November 1892 in a rich aristocratic, cultured and refined family. She was the daughter of a navy officer Sir Edmound Slade. She spent most of her childhood at her maternal grandfather's farmhouse: riding and hunting.

She was deeply impressed by Gandhi's struggle and teachings. She wanted to be his follower. Gandhiji invited her to live in the Ashram. She came and adopted a very simple life. She was also arrested and kept in Aga Khan Palace Prison for almost two years, 93 weeks to be precise.

After 'Namak Andolan', she visited many provinces. She used to send reports to other countries. Once, she was prohibited from entering Mumbai. She defied the prohibition, was arrested and imprisoned for a year.

Later on, she went on a lecture tour to England and America and explained Gandhi's point of view everywhere. She went to Bihar and worked among the people. She felt disillusioned and withdrew to the Himalayas, where she observed silence for a year. During that period, she translated Indian Scriptures, particularly the Hymns of Rig Veda into English.

During Bapu's fast, she took only one meal a day. She joined evening prayers and sang 'bhajans'. She worked as a secretary to Bapu, writing his answers and getting them corrected. She set up *'Kisan Ashram'* at Roorkee and Haridwar, and *'Gopal Ashram'* at Bhilangna valley in Tehri Garhwal. She left India in January 1959. The Government of India awarded her 'Padma Vibhushan', which was presented to her by the Indian Ambassador in Vienna. A postage stamp was also issued in her honour. She passed away on 20 July, 1982.

ॐ

[October 13, 1930]

CHI. MIRA,

I hope you have got the straying letters. I am sure they have not been intercepted, but have been delayed in transit from place to place.

It is evident, my 'scolding' as you call it, was well deserved, for you have returned in a dilapidated condition. On the top of that, you had a bad accident. Now you would be as good as your word and take full rest. I was much relieved to understand that you had been visiting the Sardar. That showed that you were well enough to travel.

I am still at the Gandiv wheel, and my rapture continues, if anything it has increased. I am spinning scientifically now, i.e., with a yard measure underneath the track of the yarn as it is drawn. I can draw 8 threads in one minute and I pull

162

at least two feet to each draw. This means 240 rounds or 300 yards per hour. But of course, I do nothing of the sort in an hour but that is not because of any defect in the Gandiv. The less output is due to breakages and consequent waste of time. But since adopting the method of concentration, breakages have very considerably reduced. I therefore often reach 200 yards per hour which for me is very good. You will publish nothing just yet of my views about the Gandiv. I want the report of those who may try at the Ashram. Most of all I want your report, if you have the leisure and the inclination to give it a trial. I know that you all have not the time that I have for these experiments. You will therefore do whatever is possible and if you think it necessary. I, having nothing else to do, may easily exaggerate the merits of a thing which I may have disregarded before as I did and which now gives comparative satisfaction.

For the past two days I have gone back to raisins and dates just to see if the cold I have had anything to do with the vegetables. Whether it is a coincidence or what, it is as good as gone today. In any event health is quite good. Weight 104.

Love.

BAPU

[PS.]

*Today I have finished the 100th hymn. Only two remain to be translated of the Hindustani hymns. This means I am nearly half through with this work.*

YERAVDA PRISON,
January 5, 1932

CHI. MIRA,

This goes as a business letter. Therefore no reference to it in the Press.

Please send me the larger size flask. It will be useful for keeping hot water, saving the labour of warders early morning.

I gave a cheque for Rs. 800 to Mahadev with instructions. I do not think it needed endorsement. See whether he has it and if it needs endorsement.

We are both well.

Love to all.

BAPU

ON THE TRAIN,
August 4, 1937

CHI. MIRA,

I am nearing Delhi. Mahadev and Pyarelal [are] with me. Hope to take the return train today, if not, tomorrow for certain.

I hope Akash will suit you equally well.

I never knew that both the Dharmavirs spun.

Did I tell you that Shanta did not go to England, her mother having practically stopped her? She is very happy with Mahadev and very helpful to him.

Balwantsinha has brought two more cows. We need still more.

Balkrishna is flourishing in Segaon. He eats freely under Dr. Batra's coaxing. He is on Kepler's malt cod-liver oil. I thought I should relax the rule about fish oils, as there were so many other restrictions. He is fast putting on weight of which he had lost much.

Rameshwari Devi is with me 3rd class, returning to Delhi. I hope you will return proof against malaria. So far as I am concerned I do not mind how long you are there, so long as you keep fit and renew your body.

I am sorry about Subhas. The enclosed for him.

Love.

BAPU

SEGAON, WARDHA,
February 3, 1939

CHI. MIRA,

Your letter from Peshawar is crowded with news. You are in the thick of it now. You must keep your health at any cost. Cover your feet well. Insist on the food you need. Do not overdo it. And do not go beyond your depth. Then all will be well.

Have no worry on my account. God will keep me on earth so long as he needs me. It is well whether I am here or elsewhere. His will, not ours, be done.

Love.

BAPU

BHANGI COLONY, NEW DELHI,
May 25, 1947

CHI. MIRA,

I have your precious letter just received, i.e., 5 o'clock. I am dictating this whilst spinning. The whole day has been spent in seeing people with a little break for rest. You need not wait to see the Vicereine. But you should proceed to Uttarkashi or Mussoorie as the case may be. Your solitude, the bracing air that you get in Mussoorie and Uttarkashi and consequent clear thinking are more precious to me than your seeing high personages or even coming to see me because I appear to be so near. That is only an appearance. I am near enough wherever you are and wherever I am physically. The rest of your letter it is unnecessary for me to touch. I approve all your programme. I am quite well, though in boiling heat. I must not think of Mussoorie or any other similar climate. My work today lies in the affected parts. If God wishes me to do his work, he would keep me well in spite of adverse climate.

Love.
BAPU

SHRIMATI MIRABEHN
P. O. RISHIKESH
DEHRA DUN DISTRICT

NEW DELHI,
June 29/30, 1947

CHI. MIRA,

I have your two wires and two letters giving me a vivid description of your experiences in Uttarkashi. The second letter is disturbing. After I commenced dictating I felt like dozing and I dozed. After the dozing was finished I got your third letter telling me about your movement to Dhanaulti. I hope that you were able, without any harm to the body, to negotiate the journey in your dilapidated condition. It grieves me to think that even Uttarkashi with all its sacred associations could do no good to your body and that you found the water there to be too heavy and the atmosphere stifling. I hope the new place will treat you better. By going to Uttarkashi you have knocked on the head and on the principle of 'once bitten twice shy'. I shall look upon every Himalayan place with suspicion. However, I am in God's hands. I shall wish neither one way nor the other. Sufficient unto the day is the good thereof. I must not think of the evil. No one knows what is really good or evil. Therefore, let us think of nothing but good. Coming to mundane matters, when I am free from here I must go to Bihar and Noakhali and I might have to go to Kashmir almost immediately. Date will be decided, I hope, inside of a week. To Hardwar I went only for a few hours to see the refugees. The weather was too hot to permit of much movement.

Blessings from

BAPU

SHRI MIRABEHN
C/O SHRI DEVDAS GANDHI
BIRLA HOUSE
MUSSOORIE

CALCUTTA,
August 20, 1947

CHI. MIRA,

Your two letters and wire. I hope you got mine at Pratap Nagar. All your letters were received.

So you have not gained by your stay in the Himalayan Hills! You are evidently unable to build up your body.

I suggest your giving up all activities including cow-keeping. What about the buildings you have erected and the ground taken? You can certainly come back to me and stay at will. Have no irons in the fire till your body is like true steel. I hold that it can be like that if the conditions are fulfilled.

I hope the examination of your heart will prove satisfactory.

I am fixed up here for the time being. Then the intention is to go to Noakhali. When that time will come I do not know.

This letter has taken me two hours to finish. There were many interruptions.

BAPU

[PS.]

*I had expressed the intention to pass my days in Pakistan, no promise.*

□

# A Letter to Adolf Hitler

If there was any centralised power and dominance, it was Hitler. He had grown so strong and punished his enemies in such a way that the other European and American countries joined hands to wipe him out. They needed a World War to end the reign of Hitler, whose some friends deccived him. Even after his death, Hitler is a power to reckon with and an emblem of fear that shakes even strong hearts and militant brains.

Adolf Hitler was born on April 20, 1899 at Braunau am Inn in Austria and died on April 30, 1945 in Berlin, Germany. He is always known as the Dictator of Nazi Germany. He ruled from 1933 to 1945.

Hitler moved from Vienna to Munich in 1913. He fought the World War-I as a soldier in the German Army. After the war, he joined German Workers' Party in 1919. In 1920, he became head of propaganda for the re-named National Socialists or Nazi Party. He became the party leader in 1921. Using unrelenting propaganda, he created a mass movement. The party's rapid growth came to climax in 1923 in Beer Hall Putsch for which he served nine months in prison. In the jail, he wrote his virulent autobiography **'Mein Kampf.'** In it he propounded anti-semitism, anti-communism and extreme German Nationalism. He advocated inequality, exalted and advocated the superiority of the 'Aryan Race'.

The economic slump of 1929 held him and renewed his inner vigour and political power.

In 1932, Hitler seriously contested for the president but lost. He entered intrigues to gain legitimate power. In 1933, Paul Von Hinderburg invited him to be the Chancellor. He became the Chancellor and adopted the title of Fuhrer, which means 'leader'. He gained dictatorial power with the Enabling Act. He suppressed opposition with the assistance of Heinrich Himmer and Joseph Goebbels. He started enacting anti-Jewish measures, which culminated in the famous holocaust. He became an ally of Benito Mussolini in the Rome-Berlin Axis. The German-Soviet Non-aggression Pact of 1939 enabled him to invade Poland and participate in the World War-II. It is said that in an underground bunker in Berlin, he married Eva Braun and the very next day they committed suicide.

Gandhi wrote three letters to Hitler. The British Government did not allow one letter to be sent. One letter of Gandhi is available and is printed here. It speaks volumes.

৪০৫

WARDHA,
December 24, 1940

DEAR FRIEND,

That I address you as a friend is no formality. I own no foes. My business in life has been for the past 33 years to enlist the friendship of the whole of humanity by befriending mankind, irrespective of race, colour or creed.

I hope you will have the time and desire to know how a good portion of humanity who have been living under the influence of that doctrine of universal friendship view your action. We have no doubt about your bravery or devotion to your fatherland, nor do we believe that you are the monster described by your opponents. But your own writings and pronouncements and those of your friends and admirers leave no room for doubt that many of your acts are monstrous and unbecoming of human dignity, especially in the estimation of men like me who believe in universal friendliness. Such are your humiliation of Czechoslovakia,

169

the rape of Poland and the swallowing of Denmark. I am aware that your view of life regards such spoliations as virtuous acts. But we have been taught from childhood to regard them as acts degrading humanity. Hence, we cannot possibly wish success to your arms.

But ours is a unique position. We resist British Imperialism no less than Nazism. If there is a difference, it is in degree. One-fifth of the human race has been brought under the British heel by means that will not bear scrutiny. Our resistance to it does not mean harm to the British people. We seek to convert them, not to defeat them on the battle-field. Ours is an unarmed revolt against the British rule. But whether we convert them or not, we are determined to make their rule impossible by non-violent non-co-operation. It is a method in its nature indefensible. It is based on the knowledge that no spoliator can compass his end without a certain degree of co-operation, willing or compulsory, of the victim. Our rulers may have our land and bodies but not our souls. They can have the former only by complete destruction of every Indian—man, woman and child. That all may not rise to that degree of heroism and that a fair amount of frightfulness can bend the back of revolt is true but the argument would be beside the point. For, if a fair number of men and women be found in India who would be prepared without any ill will against the spoliators to lay down their lives rather than bend the knee to them, they would have shown the way to freedom from the tyranny of violence. I ask you to believe me when I say that you will find an unexpected number of such men and women in India. They have been having that training for the past 20 years.

We have been trying for the past half a century to throw off the British rule. The movement of independence has been never so strong as now. The most powerful political organisation, I mean the Indian National Congress, is trying to achieve this end. We have attained a very fair measure of success through non-violent effort. We were groping for the right means to combat the most organised violence in the world which the British power represents. You have challenged it. It remains to be seen which is the better organised, the German or the British. We know what the British heel means for us and the non-European races of the world. But we would never wish to end the British rule with German aid. We have found in non-violence a force which, if organised, can without doubt match itself against a combination of all the most violent forces in the world. In non-violent technique, as I have said, there is no such thing as defeat. It is all 'do or die' without killing or hurting. It can be used practically without money and obviously without the aid of science of destruction which you have brought to such perfection. It is a marvel to me that you do not see that it is nobody's monopoly. If not the British, some other power will certainly improve upon your method and beat you with your own weapon. You are leaving no legacy to your people of which they would feel proud. They cannot take pride in a recital of cruel deed, however skilfully planned. I, therefore, appeal to you in the name of humanity to stop the war. You will lose nothing by referring all the matters of dispute between you and Great Britain to an international tribunal of your joint choice. If you attain success in the war, it will not prove that you were in the right. It will only prove that your power of destruction was greater. Whereas an award by an impartial tribunal will show as far as it is humanly possible which party was in the right.

You know that not long ago I made an appeal to every Briton to accept my method of non-violent resistance. I did it because the British know me as a friend though a rebel. I am a stranger to you and your people. I have not the courage to make you the appeal I made to every Briton. Not that it would not apply to you with the same force as to the British. But my present proposal is much simple because much more practical and familiar.

During this season when the hearts of the peoples of Europe yearn for peace, we have suspended even our own peaceful struggle. Is it too much to ask you to make an effort for peace during a time which may mean nothing to you personally but which must mean much to the millions of Europeans whose dumb cry for peace I hear, for my ears are attuned to hearing the dumb millions? I had intended to address a joint appeal to you and Signor Mussolini, whom I had the privilege of meeting when I was in Rome during my visit to England as a delegate to the Round Table Conference. I hope that he will take this as addressed to him also with the necessary changes.

I am,

Your sincere friend,

M. K. GANDHI

□

# Letters to Subhash Chandra Bose

Subhash Chandra Bose had all the inherent qualities of a true and truly great leader. Among numerous leaders, only he is known as "Netaji". He was not meek humble or submissive. He had a rare will power and confidence, intelligence and wisdom, independent ideas and views, synthetic philosophy and pragmatic insight. All these, and many other qualities combined together, made him a powerful figure which was different and worked in a different way during the prolonged struggle of India's independence. That proves him to be a born leader and revolutionary.

Subhash Chandra Bose was born on the 23rd January, 1897 at Cuttak in Orissa. He is believed to have succumbed to burn injury in a plane crash on August 18, 1945 at Taipei, Taiwan.

He was preparing in England for a career in Indian Civil Services, when the turmoil back home gave him a clarion call and on return he straightaway moved into it. Gandhiji sent him to Bengal to organise and lead movements there. The British did not like it. He was imprisoned and deported many times. He was violent by nature and favoured industrialisation which were against the thinking and philosophy of Gandhi, yet he was elected the President of the Indian National Congress twice: First in 1938 and second time against the open opposition of Gandhi in 1939. He resigned and started 'Forward Block'.

He was under house arrest when he disguised out of India, met world leaders, and carried on the struggle for independence all on his own. He raised a big army, 'Azad Hind Fauz' and moved towards India winning outer territories. His associates, the Japanese surrendered, and he had to leave the battlefield and the plane, thought to be carrying him, crashed. His death was never confirmed beyond a reasonable doubt.

The issue of his death was raised in the Indian Parliament and Prime Minister Nehru constituted a committee on 3rd December, 1955. The report could not satisfy the members and the people. Another committee was appointed in 1970 but there was no end to the controversy. Yet another committee consisting of only Justice M. K. Mukherji was appointed on the 14th May, 1999 which claimed that Netaji did not die in the plane crash and that the ashes in Renkoji Temple, Tokyo, are not that of Netaji.

Anyway, Netaji has not died, at least, for the Indians. He is alive and working, with the same zeal, enthusiasm and dedication in the heart and mind of millions, to give peace, prosperity and real freedom to his motherland.

ॐ

WARDHA,
December 20, 1929

DEAR FRIEND,

You attribute to me powers I know I do not possess. There are no-changers and pro-changers nowadays. It would be wrong on my part to interfere with the discretion of co-workers in matters outside the operations which keep them in touch with me. If there is any specific thing against any of them, I shall gladly go into it.

But whether I can be of any service or not I wish you could find a way out of this unseemly wrangling.

Yours sincerely,

M. K. G.

SUBHAS BOSE

❀   ❀   ❀

DEAR SUBHAS BABU,

You are becoming more and more an enigma to me. I want you to live up to the certificate that Deshbandhu once gave me for you. He pictured you to me as a young man of brilliant parts, singleness of purpose, great determination and above pettiness. Your conduct in Calcutta therefore grieved me, but I reconciled myself to its strangeness. But in Lahore you became inscrutable and I smelt petty jealousy. I do not mind stubborn opposition. I personally thrive on it and learn more from opponents than from friends. I therefore always welcome sincere and intelligent opposition. But in Lahore you became an obstructionist. In connection with the Bengal dispute, in your writings to the Press you were offensive and the discourteous, impatient walk-out nearly broke my heart. You should have bravely recognised the necessity and the propriety of your and other friends' exclusion. It was not aimed at you, Prakasam or Srinivasa Iyengar. It was meant merely to strengthen the hands of the young President by providing him with a cabinet that would be helpful in carrying forward the national work.

There was no question surely of distributing patronage, of placating personal interests, however high they may be. The question was one of devising measures for achieving independence in the shortest possible time. How could you, having no faith in the programme, or Prakasam, with philosophic contempt for the present programme, or Srinivasa Iyengar, with his unfathomable unbelief in Jawaharlal and Pandit Motilalji, forward the nation's work? But all the three could help by becoming sympathetic critics offering sound suggestions along their own lines. There was certainly no undemocratic procedure. If the putting of the names *en bloc* did not commend itself to the Committee, the Committee could have so expressed its opinion and that would have been also a fair measure of the strength of your

175

party. But I do not want to continue the argument. I simply write this to ask you to retrace your steps and otherwise also prove to me and those whose co-operation you would seek, the truth of the certificate issued by Deshbandhu. I do not want to change your view about anything, but I do want you to change your conduct in enforcing those views. Yours sincerely,

⊛    ⊛    ⊛

ON THE TRAIN,<br>
ADDRESS AS AT BIRLA HOUSE,<br>
NEW DELHI<br>
March 24, 1939

MY DEAR SUBHAS,

I do hope this will find you steadily progressing towards complete recovery.

I enclose herewith copy of Sarat's letter to me and my reply. If it represents also your sentiments, then and then only my suggestions are applicable. Anyway, the anarchy at the Centre should end. In accordance with your request, I am keeping absolutely silent, though pressure is being put upon me to give my opinion on the crisis.

I saw the resolution for the first time in Allahabad. It seems to me to be quite clear. The initiative lies with you. I do not know how far you are fit to attend to national work. If you are not, I think you should adopt the only constitutional course open to you.

I shall have to be in Delhi still for a few days.

Love.

BAPU

⊛    ⊛    ⊛

NEW DELHI,<br>
March 30, 1939

MY DEAR SUBHAS,

I have delayed my reply to your letter of 25th instant for the sake of having your reply to my wire. I got Sunil's wire last night. I have now got up before morning prayer time to write this reply.

Since you think that Pandit Pant's resolution was out of order and the clause relating to the Working Committee is clearly unconstitutional and *ultra vires*, your course is absolutely clear. Your choice of the Committee should be unfettered.

Your several questions on this head, therefore, do not need any answering.

Since we met in February, my opinion has become strengthened that where there are differences on fundamentals, as we agreed there were, a composite committee would be harmful. Assuming, therefore, that your policy had the backing of the majority of the A. I. C. C., you should have a Working Committee composed purely of those who believe in your policy.

Yes, I adhere to the view expressed by me at Segaon at our February meeting that I would not be guilty of being party to any self-suppression by you, as distinguished from voluntary self-effacement. Any subordination of a view which you may strongly hold as in the best interests of the country would be self-suppression. Therefore, if you are to function as President, your hands must be unfettered. The situation before the country admits of no middle course.

So far as the Gandhi-ites (to use that wrong expression) are concerned, they will not obstruct you. They will help you where they can, they will abstain where they cannot. There should be no difficulty whatsoever, if they are in a minority. They may not suppress themselves if they are clearly in a majority.

What worries me, however, is the fact that the Congress electorate is bogus and that, therefore, majority and minority lose their full meaning. Nevertheless, till the Congress stable is cleansed, we have to manage with the instrument we have for the time being. The other thing worrying me is the terrible distrust among ourselves. Joint work is an impossibility where the workers distrust one another.

I think there is no other point in your letter that needs answering.

In all you do, may you be guided by God. Do be well quickly by obeying the doctors.

Love.

BAPU

[PS.]

*So far as I am concerned, our correspondence need not be published. But you have my permission to publish it, if you think otherwise.*

MY DEAR SUBHAS,

Your letter of 6th instant has been redirected here.

I suggested a meeting of the foes to have it out among themselves without any reservation. But so much has happened since that I do not know if it is worth while. They will only swear at one another and bitterness will become more bitter. The gulf is too wide, suspicions too deep. I see no way of closing the ranks. The only way seems to me to recognise the differences and let each group work in its own manner.

I feel myself utterly incompetent to bring the warring elements together for joint work. I should hope that they can work out their policies with becoming dignity. If they do so it will be well with the country.

Pandit Pant's resolution I cannot interpret. The more I study it the more I dislike it. The framers meant well. But, it does not answer the present difficulty. You should, therefore, give it your own interpretation and act accordingly, without the slightest hesitation.

I cannot, will not, impose a Cabinet on you. You must not have one imposed on you, nor can I guarantee approval by A. I. C. C. of your Cabinet and policy. It would amount to suppression. Let the members exercise their own judgment.

If you do not get the vote, lead the opposition till you have converted the majority.

Do you know that I have stopped civil disobedience wherever I have influence? Travancore and Jaipur are glaring examples. Even Rajkot I had stopped before I came here. I repeat that I breathe violence in the air. I see no atmosphere for non-violent action. Is not the lesson of Ramdurg enough for you? In my opinion, it has done immense injury to the cause. It was, so far as I can see, premeditated. Congressmen are responsible for it as they were in Ranpur. Do you not see that we two honestly see the same thing differently and even draw opposite conclusions? How can we meet on the political platform? Let us agree to differ there and let us meet on the social, moral and municipal platform. I cannot add the economic, for we have discovered our differences on that platform also.

My conviction is that working along our lines, in our own way, we shall serve the country better than by the different groups seeking to work a common policy and common programme forged out of irreconcilable elements.

I sent you wires from Delhi about my utter inability to go to Dhanbad. Rajkot I dare not neglect.

I am well. Ba is down with malignant malaria. This is the fifth day. I brought her with me when she had already commenced it.

I wish you will conserve your health by taking decisive action, leaving the result to God. Your reference to your father is touching. I had the pleasure of meeting him.

I forget one thing. Nobody put me up against you. What I told you in Segaon was based on my own personal observations. You are wrong if you think that you have a single personal enemy among the Old Guard.

Love.

BAPU

□

# Letters to Sarojini Naidu

Sarojini Naidu, the Nightingale of India, was not only a poetess and an orator but also a great freedom fighter. She was imprisoned but never deterred, she was praised but never swept away, she created a poetic and imaginative world but never lost the solid ground of reality on which she moved. She visited both South Africa and England but remained true to her motherland and represented the country, its people, its culture and spirituality and also idealism of her life through speeches and poems collected in: "Golden Threshold", "Bird of Time' and 'Broken Wing."

Though the family of Sarojini Naidu belonged to Bengal, she was born in Hyderabad on the 13th February, 1879. Her parents were learned. Her mother used to compose poems in Bengali. Sarojini Naidu was brought up equally in Indian tradition and western literary milieu. She passed her Matriculation Examination at the tender age of 12 and next year she composed 'Lady of the Lake', a long poem of 1300 lines within six days.

The Nizam of Hyderabad sent her to England for higher studies at the age of 16 where she studied at King's College, London and Girton College, Cambridge. She returned back after three years and became famous as a poetess.

In 1898, she married a south Indian Doctor: Govind Rajulu Naidu. She had four children but lost the eldest son very early, which she could not forget till the end.

With total commitment to the cause of the nation and its freedom, she joined National Movement for Independence and moved the people with her spirited speeches in Bengali, Hindi, English, Urdu and Gujarati. She went to England to comprise the people, what had happened at Jallianwalla Bagh. She was elected Congress President in 1925 at Kanpur. In 1931, she represented Congress at the Round Table Conference in London. Her last imprisonment at the time of Quit India Movement' in 1942 lasted for three years. After independence, she was appointed the Governor of Uttar Pradesh. She departed from the world on the 12th March, 1949.

She remained associated with Gandhi and true to national cause and freedom throughout her life. She gave the epithet 'spinner' to Mahatma Gandhi: "Spinner of India's Destiny" which he liked and used as his signature in the letters to the sweet singer 'Bulbul.'

৶৹৻

SERVANTS OF INDIA SOCIETY,
POONA CITY,
February 23, 1915

MY DEAR SISTER,

What would you say of a brother who does not inquire about his sister's health, does not acknowledge her message of goodwill and who does not even send a note of sympathy on her father's death? You will believe me when I tell you that I have not had a moment's rest after our landing. I thought therefore that I would write to you on settling down somewhere. Then I heard from Mr. Gokhale just when I left for Bolpur that you had lost your father. I said to myself then that I would write to you on reaching Bolpur. But no sooner did I reach Bolpur, then I had to retrace my steps to visit the desolate home of the Society. Oh! the pity of it. And yet my Rajya Guru died as very few had the privilege of dying.

And now excuse me for the delay in writing to you. My sympathies are with you in your sorrow. You have enough philosophy in you to bear the grief that has overtaken you. Do please let me know how you are keeping.

With regards from us both,

Yours sincerely,

M. K. GANDHI

MY DEAR SISTER,

I did not reply to your last letter as I had hoped to be able at the time of replying to tell you when I was likely to visit Hyderabad. But the receipt of your booklet with the beautiful inscription in it compels me to write to you now, even though I cannot fix the date of my coming to Hyderabad.

I thank you for the inscription. Yes, Mr. Gokhale longed to have you as a full servant of India. Your acknowledgment of discipleship fills one with new hope. But of this more when we meet. For me the death of the Master has drawn me closer to him. I see him and appreciate his worth as I never did before; for the lover, the loved one never dies.

Are you keeping well in health?

I leave Madras on the 7th instant for Bombay.

My permanent address is Servants of India Society, Poona.

Mrs. Gandhi, who is with me, sends her love to you.

Yours sincerely,

M. K. GANDHI

August 7, 1929

MY DEAR PEACE-MAKER,

I have your letter giving me all the information about dogs

and daughters. I suppose you put the dogs first because they are less troublesome.

I shall be in Bombay on 11th by the Gujarat Mail, not the Kathiawar Mail which comes an hour later. I dare not stay at the Taj. I must go to Laburnum Road. Nothing will be required at Mr. Jinnah's house as I shall have taken horse's food at Laburnum Road.

You will please send me back the same day.

Lovingly yours,

MATTER-OF-FACT
(NOT MYSTIC)
SPINNER

August 8, 1932

DEAR BULBUL,

Here is a letter from Dr. Ansari which you would like to read. It is meant as much for you as for us.

You got my message about your loving gifts! This is not to invite a repetition. We are spoilt children of nature and have everything we need in the way of creature comforts.

It is naughty of Padmaja to neglect me for so long. I hope she is better. Do you hear from your bearded son? If you write to him, please give him my love.

Have the ladies there told you that Sardar is seriously studying Sanskrit? He has made much progress during the four weeks he has been at it. His application would shame a youthful student.

Love from us all.

Yours,

LITTLE MAN

SEGAON, WARDHA,
November 26, 1938

MY DEAR FLY,

Who is most distinguished daughter of Bengal and equally distinguished daughter-in-law of Andhra.

Though you are so distinguished, you are still a fly, thank God.

I have already written to Padmaja without in any way mentioning you for the journey. You are past praying for. Much love till we meet on or about 8th Dec.

Yours,

LITTLE SPINNER,

SPIDER, ETC.

SEVAGRAM, via WARDHA (C.P.),
July 18, 1941

MY DEAR SINGER,

I have been too busy seeing people to overtake even important letters like yours.

As to Mr. Munshi, my position is clear. When he could not conform to the explicit resolution of the Congress on internal disorders, I had no option but to advise him to leave. I cannot be held responsible for what he does after severing his connection with the Congress. Those who know me understand that such influence as I can exert on Shri Munshi must still be on the side of non-violence. Those who do not trust me impute motives to me which I can only disprove by my conduct.

As to the workers, they are bound by the Congress resolution I have quoted in my letter to Shri Munshi. The Congress policy binds them to non-violence in the struggle with the Government as also in dealing with communal riots and the like. Is not this crystal clear?

Love.

Yours,

SPINNER

DEAR SINGER,

I agree that I should move about if I can. But I must repudiate the charge that my judgment goes astray by my being cut off from outside contact. I have breathed not a word about the undue deaths. And in my letter to Padmaja, I simply told her what the papers had suggested. Mark my extraordinary care in avoiding all public reference without testing the truth of the allegations through no less an authority than sober Padmaja. I therefore accept your apology in anticipation.

Love.

SPINNER

□

# Letters to C. Raja Gopalachari

C. Raja Gopalachari, popularly known as Rajaji, was a man of great moral character. He was one of the earlier associates of Mahatma Gandhi. He was born in 1878 and died in 1972. He lived a long life of 94 years because of the inner discipline that he showed in all his deeds.

Chakravarti Raja Gopalachari was the Premier of Madras during 1937 and 39. He was a reputed lawyer who became a Minister in the Interim Government of India in 1946-47. Then, he was appointed the Governor of West Bengal in 1947-48. But he was called back to become the first 'Indian' Governor General of India. He held the office from 1948 to 50, when the Indian Constitution was adopted and the first President of India was elected.

Raja Gopalachari became the Minister for Home for a brief period and then the Chief Minister of Madras from 1952-54. He founded **Swatantra Party** and opposed Nehru's programmes. He wrote two scholarly books: the Intrepretations of the Ramayana and the Mahabharata. His daughter Lakshmi was married to the youngest son of Mahatma Gandhi, Devadas Gandhi in 1933.

Raja Gopalachari contributed to the struggle for independence in three ways: individual contribution, as co-ordinator and as a follower of Gandhi and in the implementation of the programmes of the Congress.

He maintained a very cordial relation with all the persons who came into his contact. He was an organised person, hence, it was easier for him to organise people. That is the reason he did justice to whatever post and responsibility he was given. His insight and inside knowledge came handy at every turn. He remained totally a non-controversial person. He was so much attached to the ideals that when he found Nehru deviating from the path, he founded **Swatantra Party**.

Despite all these, he was not a mass leader. He held many higher posts both in the party and in the governments. He lost contact with the people. He could not visit and guide them at regular intervals and in their sufferings.

☙❧

C/o M. MAHOMED ALI,
"COMRADE" OFFICE,
DELHI,
September 15, 1924

DEAR RAJAGOPALACHARI,

I have been constantly thinking of you ever since the reading of your letter. How is it that you do not see the necessity as clearly as I do of the step I have taken? I agree with you that it is better to leave the Congress if we cannot enforce our programme. The difficulty is to know how. I cannot help feeling that we must not embarrass the Swarajists. They are supplying a felt want. They do represent a large section of people who want petty relief. Shall we obstruct them? Ours is predominantly a spiritual activity. Its strength is developed unperceived and not by merely debating and vote-taking. I am still not clearly expressing myself. I have simply set forth one argument out of many for the course I have taken and advised for adoption by us all. Somehow or other I feel the absolute correctness of the step even though I cannot demonstrate it to your satisfaction. I know how difficult it must be for you and others suddenly to accommodate yourselves to these sudden changes. But how shall I help myself ! I know I am putting an undue strain upon the loyalty and the faith of co-workers. But is it not better that I should do that rather than that I should suppress the clear voice within? Of what use should I be if I once stifled that monitor? But this merely by the way.

BAPU

MY DEAR C.R.

I have your letter. I wish you will cease to worry about me. I can only give you my assurance that I shall do nothing wilfully to impair my health. But you know my nature. I cannot exist without dietetic experiment if I am fixed up at any place for any length of time. You know too that it has always been my intense longing to revert to fruit and nut diet or at least a milkless diet if I at all could. I find now that I can easily do so and so I have done it. Now that I can pull on with it, it would be difficult for me to go back to milk until I am satisfied that it is not possible to do without milk. I can only tell you that I shall not do anything obstinately. In accordance with Dr. Muthu's instructions I am not having the blood-pressure taken at all, but I am flourishing.

I discovered in Kathiawar that I could bring my voice to almost the original pitch without fatigue and without any discomfort. It was a well-thought-out, very rapidly delivered speech lasting for full one hour, and there was no trace of exhaustion after it. Surely, that was some test of my progress. And I was able to talk, not merely attend committee meetings for two nights, successively lasting up to 11 o'clock.

About work too, I cannot say that I am not doing very strenuous work, but it is not beyond my capacity.

What has given Lakshmi her fever? I hope that she is all right now.

188

I hope to send you Rs. 5,000/- for untouchability work soon.
BAPU

MY DEAR C. R.,

I was deeply pained to learn that in spite of repeated requests by letter and telegraph, you had failed to send your yarn subscription for the A.I.S.A. If the salt loses its savour, etc., etc. We might as well shut up shop if the tallest partner in the business is proved guilty of gross negligence. Do please send your yarn.

My experiment goes on merrily.

How are you and your prohibition work?

Yours,

BAPU

ASHRAM,
January 20, 1930

MY DEAR C. R.,

I had your letter. But I am so immersed in work that I have no time to attend to correspondence to my satisfaction.

I cannot agree that any purpose can be served by my touring. And what matters if those who believe in Councils enter them? We shall not prevent them even if we entered upon a hurricane campaign. It is for me and should be for you enough that the Congress is no longer interested in the legislatures. Touring for that purpose can only create bad blood. Vallabhbhai too agrees.

What I am doing is to think hard about civil disobedience. I have some idea of what I want to do. This much seems to me to be clear that civil disobedience must not be started under the Congress aegis, it must be started by me. Further

I have not yet been able to see. I want you to come here a few days before 14th Feb. I am asking Jawaharlal to do likewise.

I hope you are keeping well in health.

Yours,

BAPU

[PS.]

*Mahadev is taking 7 days' fast for peace of mind and Durga for health. They are both doing well.*

ASHRAM,
January 27, 1930

MY DEAR C.R.,

I cannot give you the letter I would love to. Every ounce of energy is taken up in attending to the details of life here.

I do not still see the necessity of touring. In view of the impending C.D. I do not want to create occasions for other resistances. Let the critics have a clear board as far as platform propaganda is concerned. More of this when we meet. I want you to be here at least on the 12th if not much earlier. I want you to understand me of today as thoroughly as you can.

Yes, I wrote to Srinivasa, Satyamurti and Subhas. S.N. has sent me a book of choice adjectives in reply. S.M. has sent an argumentative apology. Subhas's is a good reply. Anyway I am glad I wrote to them.

I feel that I have now a scheme of effective C.D. The picture is not yet complete. But I think I am nearing completion. I am thinking of nothing else. You must keep your health in full working order.

What a strange letter from *The Hindu*? Yet it did not surprise me.

Yours,

BAPU

DEAR C.R.,

I had your letter.

You are going through a terrible trial. But I know that in the midst of it all you can remain cheerful and unruffled. I would not think of tearing you away from Papa. So long therefore as she needs your personal nursing, I have no doubt that your duty is to be by her.

What shall I write to you about the dramatic developments? I hope your reasoning fully endorses the decision. I have personally not a shadow of a doubt about it. I wish you would be able to attend the next meeting of the Working Committee, if I am free till then. I expect still greater dramatic developments now. But I feel that all will be well and as satyagrahis we have no business to want to peep into the future. We must simply take care of the present and be sure of the future.

BAPU

SYT. C. RAJAGOPALACHARI
C/O SYT. A. V. RAMAN
LLOYD CORNER
ROYAPETTAH (MADRAS)

ON THE FRONTIER DOWN MAIL,
August 28, 1931

DEAR C.R.,

What shall I write to you? Do you know that not a day has passed but I have thought of you and also felt the need of your presence? But I was not to have it and as ill luck will have it, I cannot have even a few words with you before sailing. There are two men whom I would like by my side in London, you and Jawaharlal. But I feel that even if both of you were available I must not have you by me. Somehow or other I do feel that you will both be helping me like the

191

others by being here. Only your presence with me will have lightened my burden. But I must bear the Cross alone and to the fullest extent. When I think of myself with all my limitations and ignorance I sink in utter despair but I rise out of it immediately, as I think and feel that it is God within Who is moving me and using me as His instrument. He will give me the right word at the right moment. That does not mean that I shall make no mistakes. But I have come to believe that God as it were purposely makes us commit mistakes if only to humble us. I know that this is a dangerous belief which can be utilised to justify any error. But I have no doubt about its correctness in respect of all unconscious errors. But this is not a letter to air my philosophy. This is written to ask you to give me through weekly letters, sent even by air mail, what I cannot get through your presence. I would like you also to write for *Young India* every week. I do not think there is any legal necessity for advertising a new editor during my temporary absence. If there is a legal necessity I would like you to wear the editorial mantle.

I would like you to prepare a rejoinder to the Madras Government's reply to the Madras charge-sheet and bring the latter to date and send your rejoinder to the Sardar.

By way of preliminary send me by air mail your detailed reflections on what you expect me to do in London. Copies of whatever you send by air mail should be sent through the usual weekly service.

How is Papa? I do hope she is better.

SEGAON,
August 2, 1937

MY DEAR C. R.,

Here is an interesting cutting for you.

*Harijan* is becoming a weekly letter to the Congress Ministers. You should therefore ask Ramanathan to put before you such things that you should read. You must not wear yourself out.

I do hope you won't pay the Members for twelve months. I should regard [as enough] Rs. 2 per day whilst the Assembly is sitting plus 3rd class travelling and actual out-of-pocket for coolies and tonga not exceeding Rs. 2. But you know best.

Do read the leading article in the current *Harijan*.

Let Lakshmi write for you. I don't expect you to write to me yourself. Am off to see the Viceroy on his invitation, the cause is the mere pleasure of meeting.

Love.

Blessings from

BAPU

August 6, 1937

MY DEAR C. R.,

What nonsense! Why should you feel sorry or disappointed because I hold certain views about salaries? I do not at all resent your not enforcing them. I have said, my views need not be accepted if found unworkable. We all marvel at the way you are managing things there. You have approached your task with faith and religious zeal. You must not feel the slightest disappointment. You know my deepest feeling. Then why should you worry? I hope you will be able to spare yourself for 17th. My prayers and best wishes are with you always.

The talk with the Viceroy was formal though quite friendly.

Devdas was looking well.

Love.

BAPU

MY DEAR C. R.,

I had two hours and a half with friend Jinnah yesterday. The talk was cordial but not hopeful, yet not without hope. I must not enter into the details of the conversation, but he complained bitterly of Hindi having been imposed in particular areas of Madras in primary schools. What is exactly the position? Are Mussalman boys affected? Please send me as early a reply as possible and one that I could publicly use.

I had a long chat with Jawaharlal about the Communist Party. I think we understand each other better than before on this particular question. He says [in] the Communist Party's programme, there is no violence, there is no secrecy. Why should it [be] banned therefore as such? If any communist or party resorts to violence openly or secretly or incites to violence they must be dealt with not because of allegiance to a particular party, but because of violence. Thus the author of the writing that you showed me can clearly be dealt with under law, not because there is a ban on the Communist [Party] but because the writing itself has a criminal taint. Have you anything against this argument? If the ban is lifted, what will happen?

I hope you have received the official reply from Subhas. It enables you to deal with your correspondent.

Love.

BAPU

[September 25, 1944]

MY DEAR C. R.,

If you are satisfied that my letter of yesterday is the last word you should do the following:

1. You should ask Jinnah to see you. He told me he had nothing against you, etc. If Bhulabhai has thoroughly

194

understood the position he too may see Jinnah. You may both offer to see him together.

2.  I attach great importance to the legal opinion on Jinnah's interpretation of August Resolution.

3.  Consider the following letter to Jinnah:

"MY DEAR QUAID-E-AZAM,

Yesterday's talk leads me to inflict this letter on you for which please forgive me.

I see force in your argument that the para in my letter of yesterday can be interpreted to touch the League sensitiveness. Please therefore read the following instead:

'Any member or group from among the Congress or the League members will be free to resort to direct action including C. R. in the course of the campaign of Independence.'

BAPU

❀ ❀ ❀

POONA,
March 11, 1946

MY DEAR C. R.,

It is just 6.15 a. m. I am to be off to Bombay by 7.30 a. m.

If we discover a mistake, must we continue it? We began making love in English—a mistake. Must it express itself only by repeating the initial mistake? You have cake and eat it also.

Love is love under a variety of garbs—even when the lovers are dumb. Probably it is fullest when it is speechless. I had thought, under its gentle unfelt compulsion, you will easily glide into Hindustani and thus put the necessary finishing touch to your service of Hindustani. But let it be as you will, not I.

I do not like your despondence. You have to be thoroughly well. Why not come to me? I hope to return in five or six days.

This *tamasha* will vanish leaving the water of life cleaner for the agitation. If it does not, what then?

*Anbudan.*

BAPU

❀ ❀ ❀

POONA,<br>March 17, 1946

MY DEAR C. R.,

Your dear letter. The Tamil lesson is good. I hope I shall not forget *anbu* and *ambu*. Does not the latter also mean lotus? What is the meaning of *anbudan*? Or is the final letter 'm'?

You are not old, and you must not feel old. You must correct the stomach. So you are so pessimistic as to think that 49 years won't be enough to see the wise people become foolish!

When are you coming to Poona?

*Romba anbudan.*

BAPU

□

# Letters to G.D. Birla

Ghanshyam Das Birla was a doyen of the Indian Industry. He laid the foundation, built a palace then created and established an empire, known as Birla Empire. His vehement success was enough to fascinate and lure other entrepreneurs to build similar empires. In no time, India became a country of corporates and big business houses. He united them and founded the "Federation of Indian Chamber of Commerce," popularly known as FICCI.

Birla was a multi-faceted person and had a multi-dimensional personality. He was influenced by Gandhi, was very close to him and was his advisor to economic policies. He was the most important contributor to the Indian National Congress. But he is known more and revered a lot for 'Birla Mandirs' that he got constructed all over India first, then all over the world along with Birla Dharmashalas.

A native of Pilani, G.D. Birla was born on the 10th of April, 1894. He was the grandson of a traditional money-lender Marwari, Shri Shiva Narayan Birla. During the first World War, he entered the business world with a cotton mill, then shifted to Bengal, the largest producer region of Jute, with a Jute-Mill. During the 1930s, he shifted his eyes and opened sugar and paper mills. He acquired European companies and ventured into Tea and Textile industries. At his calculated pace, he measured out the Cement, Chemical, Rayon and Steel Industries.

Birla's another great contribution lies in the field of education. He started many educational institutions with different aims and objects, including Birla Institute of Technology and Sciences. The angles of his ideas shifted and there was a chain of Birla planetariums and hospitals.

Birla provided everything that the people needed. There lies his greatness.

His Birla house in Delhi was the abode of Gandhi. It is the place where Nathuram Godse shot at Gandhi during the evening prayer congregation. The building is now a national heritage with **'Gandhi Smriti Sangrahalaya'**. It possesses and shows Gandhi to visitors. The library provides them insight into the great Mahatma and his splendid deeds.

ಋಿ಄ಌ

Shravana Shukla 8,
July 28, 1925

BHAI GHANSHYAMDASJI,

I have your letter. I am convinced that without Malaviyaji and Shraddhanandji Hindu-Muslim unity is impossible to achieve. I can only guide and when stray quarrels take place, do something about them if I can. My task is that of a scavenger: to work for and ensure cleanliness. When the time comes to work out a settlement it will be most necessary to consult Malaviyaji and others.

Yours,

MOHANDAS GANDHI

Shravana Krishna 11
[August 14, 1925]

BHAI GHANSHYAMDASJI,

I have your letter. I hope Father is now well. I have written what I could for Pandit Sunderlalji The problem of the Hindu-Muslim tension is getting more and more difficult each day. What I have suggested will provide a basis for what you want. If the Delhi riot could be thoroughly probed it could become the basis for further work. I firmly believe that in the end many leaders will have to lay down their lives.

Yours,

MOHANDAS

Shri Ghanshyamdas Birla
137, CANNING STREET
CALCULTTA

SABARMATI,
Thursday [After February 11, 1926]
BHAI GHANSHYAMDASJI,

I have your telegram and letter. I am glad that your mind is at peace. I can now hope that you will not fall into the snare of a second marriage.

I do not see any possibility of my going to South Africa.

Yours,

MOHANDAS GANDHI

THE ASHRAM
February 7, 1928
BHAI GHANSHYAMDASJI,

It certainly causes anxiety when there is no letter from you. Drugs are bound to make one feel tired. The primary therapy in my view is complete fasting. I entertain no fear on this score. Fasting can never cause harm and it should be resorted to not for a day or two but for ten or fifteen days. If you decide to fast here you must come and stay here. There are one or two friends well versed in the science of fasting whom we can summon. We have the accommodation. The air at this time is good. If you would rather have the fasting specialists go to Pilani, that too could be arranged.

It is my firm view that you should not go to Delhi. I am going to write to Malaviyaji and Lalaji right away. I had published an appeal in *Young India* and *Navajivan* in connection with the Hakim Ajmal Khan memorial. I want you and your friends to contribute. If you do not wish to advance any more moneys, I can, if you permit, take away a large chunk from the Rs. 75,000/- you have given me, leaving it to you whether you want your name to be published or not. If you feel I ought not to draw upon the sum, please do not hesitate to let me know.

Do not be scared by the reports about my health appearing in the Press. There is really no cause for anxiety. The doctors do scare one, but I am not perturbed.

Yours,

MOHANDAS

SATYAGRAHA ASHRAM,
SABARMATI,
February 8, 1928

BHAI GHANSHYAMDASJI,

I have your letter. One can make digestible things with oil in them, but this sort of experiment cannot be carried out from a distance. In the present situation, fasting is the most important and the best remedy for you. I have not the slightest doubt about it.

Yours,

MOHANDAS

January 14, 1929

BHAISHRI GHANSHYAMDASJI,

I have your wire as also your letter. I am going to Sind towards the end of the month in connection with the Lalaji memorial. Have you made any collection in Calcutta?

As regards the dairy, I had suggested to you the name of someone from Madras. Did you write to him? If he is not considered suitable I can suggest another name.

As to the Khadi Bhandar, we must not forget the purpose for which it is intended. We must not pursue a purely commercial aim. The Bhandar should be run for future good.

I am well. My diet these days is 15 tolas of almond milk, 14 tolas of bread (soaked), vegetables and tomatoes, 4 tolas of linseed oil and 2 tolas of flour paste in the morning. I have given up fruit here. I have gained 1 1/2 lb. in a week. I feel energetic.

Yours,

MOHANDAS

November 26, 1946

CHI. GHANSHYAMDAS,

You know I am staying at Srirampur all by myself, with only Prof. Nirmal Kumar Bose and Parasuram as my companions. The people with whom I am putting up are gentlemen. There is only one Hindu family in the entire village, the rest are all Muslims. They all stay widely separated from each other. The hundreds of villages here do not maintain much contact with each other through any conveyance after the water dries up. The result is that work is possible only on foot. Therefore, only desperadoes, hooligans, or able-bodied men can maintain contact among themselves. I am living in one such village at present and intend to spend more time in another village similar to this. It is my intention to stay on here so long as the Hindus and Muslims do not start living together as sincere friends. God alone can keep man's resolve unshaken. At the moment I have forgotten Delhi, Sevagram, Uruli and Panchgani. My only desire is to do or die. This will test my non-violence, too. I have come here determined to emerge successful from this ordeal. If you are anxious to see me, then you can come over here. I personally do not see any necessity for it. If you wish to send a messenger to know something or carry letters by hand, you can do so.

I am not going into the Constituent Assembly; it is not quite necessary either. Jawaharlal, Sardar, Rajendra Babu, Rajaji, Maulana—any of these or all five can go—or Kripalani.

Send them the message.

If it is possible to arrange for a sitting of the Constituent Assembly only with the help of the military, then it is better not to have it. If it can be arranged peacefully, then the laws can be framed only for the participating Provinces. Let us see what the future of the police and the military will be. We have also to see what the Muslim majority Provinces will do, and what is to be done in the Provinces where Muslims are in minority, how the British Government will conduct itself, and how the Princes will react. I believe the State Paper of May 16 will probably have to be changed. The job is complicated enough, if we want to work independently. I have only given an indication of how I view the problem.

Friends will also do well to bear in mind that what I am doing here is not in the name of the Congress. Nor is there any thought of associating it with this work. What I am doing is only from my personal view of non-violence. Anybody, if he so desires, can publicly oppose my work. That in fact is his right; it may even be his duty. Therefore, whosoever wishes to do anything or say anything, let him do so fearlessly. If anybody wants to warn me of anything, let him do that too.

Please send a copy of this to Sardar so that he may tell the others named above. Or you can get copies made and send them to the five friends yourself.

Do express whatever you wish to. Write to me direct so that I may reply. Pyarelal, Sushila, etc., all are in different villages. Pyarelal has been ill since yesterday. I hope you are all right.

Blessings from

BAPU

CHI. GHANSHYAMDAS,

I sent you a letter through Sushila. But I have been upset somewhat by Sardar's letter. Devdas's letter is still ringing in my ears. I do not remember what I wrote to you, for I have not kept a copy of it. All I wish today to write is that you should give up your attitude of neutrality. Sardar is quite clear in his mind that what I look upon as my dharma is really *adharma*. Devdas of course has written as much. I have great faith in Sardar's judgment. I have faith in Devdas's judgment too, but then, though grown up, in my eyes he is still a child. This cannot be said of Sardar. Kishorelal and Narahari too are grown-ups; but it is not difficult for me to understand their opposition. The link between you and me is your faith that my life is pure, spotless and wholly dedicated to the performance of dharma. If that is not so, very little else remains. I would, therefore, like you to take full part in this discussion, though not necessarily publicly—for I certainly do not want your business to suffer. But if I am conducting myself sinfully, it becomes the duty of all friends to oppose me vehemently. A satyagrahi may end up as a *duragrahi* if he comes to regard untruth as truth—that being the only distinction between the two. I believe that is not the case with me; but that means little, for after all I am not God. I can commit mistakes; I have committed mistakes; this may prove to be my biggest at the fag end of my life. If that be so, all my well-wishers can open my eyes if they oppose me. If they do not I shall go from here even as I am. Whatever I am doing here is as a part of my *yajna*. There is nothing I do knowingly which is not a part and parcel of that *yajna*. Even the rest I take is as a part of that *yajna*.

I am dictating this with a mud-pack over my eyes and abdomen. Shortly afterwards I shall be going to the evening prayer meeting. This business about Manu is taking up a lot of my time, but I do not mind it because even her presence here is for the sake of that *yajna*. Her test constitutes a part of that *yajna*. I may not be able to explain it to you—that is a different matter. The point I must make my friends grasp is this: When I take Manu in my lap, do I do so as a purehearted father or as a father who has strayed from the path of virtue? What I am doing is nothing new to me; in thought I have done it over the last 50 years; in action, in varying degrees, over quite a number of years. Even if you sever all connection with me, I would not feel hurt. Just as I want to stick to my dharma, you have to stick to yours.

To come to another matter, the Hindu weavers here—known as tantis—are very angry. Their spinning-wheels and houses have been for the most part burnt. If they do not get a supply of yarn they have either to be idle or take to earth work as labourers. The officer in charge here tells me that the Government cannot provide them yarn unless the Central Government helps. I told him I might be able to obtain the needed supply if they were prepared to pay for it. He has agreed. Can you supply the yarn? If yes, then how much, when and at what price? Will it be necessary to obtain the sanction of the Interim Government? Please let me know in detail.

Blessings from

BAPU

□

# Letters to Rabindra Nath Tagore

Though, the spiritual self of Rabindra Nath Tagore left the physical body on 7th August, 1941, with his poetic expressions and prose writings he left behind a treasure of ideas for the human beings so that they can be refined, sublime and spiritual. Tagore was an artist, musician, poet, dramatist, novelist, story-teller, critic, editor, linguist, social worker, political activist and educationist. He was everywhere, both directly and indirectly, engrossed and aloof. He gave us our national song: "Jana Gana Mana".

Ravindra Nath Thakur was born in a rich Bengali family as the son of Maharishi Devendra Nath Thakur on 7th May, 1861. His father was a religious person and social worker and an artist also.

His learning of different books on different subjects was completed mostly at home. His brother Jyotindra Nath played piano and he composed poem both in Bengali and English on the tunes. He stayed for a short time in Ahmedabad with his brother Satyendra Pal who was the first Indian I.C.S. He went to England but returned back soon. Studied the life of Bengal well and painted it in his books.

He morally supported the Non-Cooperation Movement of Mahatma Gandhi. He returned the 'Knighthood' given by the British. Gandhi respected him so much that he used to call him

'Gurudeva'. Tagore is known only by that as 'Gurudeva'. They had immense faith in the inner ability of one another. There are many popular anecdotes related to them.

He was injured deeply at both the World Wars. He opposed and wrote against the wars. He was given Nobel Prize for Literature on his poetic creation "Gitanjali."

ఐఱ

September 20, 1932

DEAR GURUDEV,

This is early morning 3 o'clock of Tuesday. I enter the fiery gate at noon. If you can bless the effort, I want it. You have been to me a true friend because you have been a candid friend often speaking your thoughts aloud. I had looked forward to a firm opinion from you one way or the other. But you have refused to criticise. Though it can now only be during my fast I will yet prize your criticism, if your heart condemns my action. I am not too proud to make an open confession of my blunder, whatever the cost of the confession, if I find myself in error. If your heart approves of the action I want your blessing. It will sustain me. I hope I have made myself clear.

My love.

M. K. GANDHI

[PS.] 10.30 a.m.

*Just as I was handing this to the Superintendent, I got your loving and magnificent wire. It will sustain me in the midst of the storm I am about to enter. I am sending you a wire.*

*Thank you.*

M.K.G.

DEAR GURUDEV,

I received your letter only just now. There is a campaign of vilification of me going on. My remarks on the Bihar calamity were a good handle to beat me with. I have spoken about it at many meetings. Enclosed is my considered opinion. I see from your statement that we have come upon perhaps a fundamental difference. But I cannot help myself. I do believe that super-physical consequences flow from physical events. How they do so, I do not know.

If after reading my article, you still see the necessity of publishing your statement, it can be at once published either here or there just as you desire. I hope you are keeping well.

Yours sincerely,

M. K. GANDHI

[PS.]

*The last lines are disgracefully written but I was tired out and half asleep. Please forgive. If I am to catch the post today, I may not wait to make a fair copy.*

□

# A letter to F.D. Roosevelt

Franklin Delano Roosevelt was the 32nd President of the United States during the period of turmoil and 2nd World War, from 1933 to 45. He was the cousin of Theodore Roosevelt, popularly known as Teddy Roosvelt, the 26th President of the U.S.

Roosevelt was born on January 30, 1882 at Hyde park, New York, U.S. and died on April 12, 1945 at Warm Spring.

He was lured to join politics by the grand achievements of his cousin. He became active in the Democratic Party. In 1905, he was married to Eleanor Roosevelt, who became active in politics after her husband's polio attack in 1920. She was a valued adviser. They had five children.

He served in the New York Senate from 1910 to 13 and as U.S. Assistant secretary of the Navy from 1913 to 20, when he was elected by the Democrats as their Vice Presidential candidate.

As the governor of New York from 1929 to 33, he set up the first state relief agency in the U.S. In 1932, he won the Democratic presidential nomination with the help of James Farley. He announced, "The only thing we have to fear is fear itself."

Congress passed most of the changes he sought in his New Deal programme during the Ist 100 days of his term. He was re-elected overwhelmingly in 1936. U.S. was badly hit by the recession but Roosevelt concentrated more on the ensuing World War-II.

He developed the lend-lease programme to aid U.S. **allies,** especially Britain and the Soviet Union. He met Churchill **and** Joseph Stalin to form war policy at Tehran in 1943, and again at Yalta in 1945. Despite declining health, he won re-election for a fourth term but served only briefly before his death.

Despite his legendary changeable stands, Roosevelt was a true Democrat and worked for the betterment of his people even at the heavy cost of war and deaths.

ৡৄঌ

SEVAGRAM, via WARDHA (INDIA),
July 1, 1942

DEAR FRIEND,

I twice missed coming to your great country. I have the privilege [of] having numerous friends there both known and unknown to me. Many of my countrymen have received and are still receiving higher education in America. I know too that several have taken shelter there. I have profited greatly by the writings of Thoreau and Emerson. I say this to tell you how much I am connected with your country. Of Great Britain I need say nothing beyond mentioning that in spite of my intense dislike of British rule, I have numerous personal friends in England whom I love as dearly as my own people. I had my legal education there. I have therefore nothing but good wishes for your country and Great Britain. You will therefore accept my word that my present proposal, that the British should unreservedly and without reference to the wishes of the people of India immediately withdraw their rule, is prompted by the friendliest intention. I would like to turn into goodwill the ill will which, whatever may be said to the contrary, exists in India towards Great Britain and thus enable the millions of India to play their part in the present war.

My personal position is clear. I hate all war. If, therefore, I could persuade my countrymen, they would make a most effective and decisive contribution in favour of an honourable peace. But I know that all of us have not a living faith in non-violence. Under foreign rule however we can make no effective contribution of any kind in this war, except as helots.

The policy of the Indian National Congress, largely guided by me, has been one of non-embarrassment to Britain, consistently with the honourable working of the Congress, admittedly the largest political organisation, of the longest standing in India. The British policy as exposed by the Cripps mission and rejected by almost all parties has opened our eyes and has driven me to the proposal I have made. I hold that the full acceptance of my proposal and that alone can put the Allied cause on an unassailable basis. I venture to think that the Allied declaration that the Allies are fighting to make the world safe for freedom of the individual and for democracy sounds hollow so long as India and, for that matter, Africa are exploited by Great Britain and America has the Negro problem in her own home. But in order to avoid all complications, in my proposal I have confined myself only to India. If India becomes free, the rest must follow, if it does not happen simultaneously.

In order to make my proposal foolproof I have suggested that, if the Allies think it necessary, they may keep their troops, at their own expense in India, not for keeping internal order but for preventing Japanese aggression and defending China. So far as India is concerned, we must become free even as America and Great Britain are. The Allied troops will remain in India during the war under treaty with the free Indian Government that may be formed by the people of India without any outside interference, direct or indirect.

It is on behalf of this proposal that I write this to enlist your active sympathy.

I hope that it would commend itself to you.

Mr. Louis Fischer is carrying this letter to you.

If there is any obscurity in my letter, you have but to send me word and I shall try to clear it.

I hope finally that you will not resent this letter as an intrusion but take it as an approach from a friend and well-wisher of the Allies.

I remain,

Yours sincerely,

M. K. GANDHI

□

# Letters to S. Radhakrishnan

The dream of a philosopher king came to be true when Dr. S. Radhakrishanan became the President of India, the head of all the three wings of Army: Infantry, Air and Navy. There is no equal to this philosopher king in any other country of the world. No one combines Indian spiritualism and western materialism, and none has explained and expressed so well besides being the head of the largest democracy of the world as Radhakrishnan did.

He had not only studied everything available and analysed them but had also exquisitely expressed them before the students and scholars of many countries. He was not only a thinker and writer but also a revered teacher; he was not only an administrator but a person who saved and gave energy and vitality through his words and sound. It is no wonder that his birthday, the 5th of September is celebrated all over the country as Teacher's Day.

Oxford praised him in the following language: "Though, the Indian preacher had the marvellous power to wear magic web of thought, imagination and language, the real greatness of his sermon resides in some indefinable spiritual quality which arrests attention, moves the heart and lifts up into an ample air."

With that Indian spirituality at the core, he worked as "Spading Professor of Eastern Religion and Ethics" at Oxford from 1936 to 39.

On his return, he was given the coveted chair of Vice-Chancellor of Benares Hindu University which he held for a long time from 1939 to 48. He led a Delegation to UNESCO and remained the Ambassador to Soviet Union till 1954 and the Chairperson of the General Assembly of UNESCO. The next ten years were spent in association with Dr. Rajendra Prasad as the Vice-president. He was awarded India's highest civilian award 'Bharat ratna' in 1953. He became the President of India in 1962.

During all these periods, he had been writing splendid books like: *Hindu View of Life; The Present Crisis of Faith; Ideal View of Life; Religion and Culture* and *Our Heritage*, etc. He departed from the world on April 17, 1975 at the age of 87.

Dr. S. Radhakrishnan is the name of the person who transgressed the Southern and Northern concept. He became fragrance and spread from East to West. He had splendid control over both the depth and height. His writing amply proves it.

ॐ

THE ASHRAM,
SABARMATI,
April 6, 1928

DEAR FRIEND,

I thank you for your kind letter. Nothing is yet certain about the proposed European visit. It is difficult for me to make up my mind.

As to the article you want, I would ask you to take pity on me. I am so thoroughly washed out and have to give so much time to *Young India* and *Navajivan* that I have very little left for managing any more writing.

Your sincerely,

M. K. GANDHI

PROF. S. RADHAKRISHNAN
49/I.C. HARISH MUKERJI RD.

213

BHAWANIPUR

CALCUTTA

DEAR SIR RADHAKRISHNAN,

I have your two letters for which many thanks.

Having yielded to you I cannot interfere with your announcement. Please do what you think best. Do however spare me the degree. These honours must be reserved for those who really deserve them. How can a law-breaker be a doctor of laws? But you may treat the occasion for donations either to the University or Harijan Sevak Sangh or A.I.S.A.

I am glad I wrote to you about young Jasani's conversation. I could not believe it. He is a good man but the foreign medium has often resulted in ludicrous misunderstandings.

Yours sincerely,

M. K. GANDHI

SRI. S. RADHAKRISHNAN
30 EDWARD ELLIOTS' ROAD
MYLAPORE, MADRAS

SRIRAMPUR,
December 17, 1946

DEAR DR. RADHAKRISHNAN,

Om Prakash gave me your letter yesterday. My congratulations on your decision. I had expected nothing less of you. You will be in charge as long as you are needed there.

I never dreamt of any of the brothers being Pro-Vice-Chancellor or holding any of the high offices in the University or even any office whatsoever except it be required in its interest. They should all be mute servants. Perhaps you have seen my article on the subject in *Harijan*.

Dr. Shyamaprasad is an ideal man for the post. Only I wish he was as sober a Hindu Sabha man as he is an able and learned administrator. You may show this to him. You are calling him to no easy job.

As to your last paragraph, the less said the better. I am on the anvil.

Yours sincerely,

M. K. GANDHI

□

# Letters to Jaiprakash Narayan

Jaiprakash Narayan, popularly known as JP, renewed his status, name and fame by leading a peaceful 'Total Revolution' in 1970s that resulted in the defeat of Mrs. Indira Gandhi. He was a true patriot and dedicated his whole life to the nation. He actively participated in the National Movement for Independence. As a recognition to his deeds and accomplishments, he was posthumously awarded the 'Bharat Ratna', the highest civilian award of the country in 1998. Earlier he was given 'Magsasay Awards' in 1965 for his public service.

JP was born on the 11th of October, 1902 at Sitab Diyara, a village in the Ballia District of Uttar Pradesh. He studied at Collegiate School and Patna College.

In 1920, JP married Prabhavati Devi. She followed his footprints and became an independent activist in her own way and right. (Gandhiji wrote her more letters than JP. Two of them are being given here.) On Gandhi's request, she stayed at his Ashram while JP continued his studies.

In 1922, JP went to the United States and studied at the University of California/ Iowa Wisconsin-Madison/ Ohio.

After returning to India, he joined Indian National Congress in 1929. He won fame during the Quit India Movement.

After Independence, he left Congress and formed Socialist Party which became Praja Socialist Party. In 1954, he joined Vinoba

Bhave's Sarvodaya movement and its Bhoodan campaign. In 1977, he called for the union of the opposition and formed and led Janta Party to victory in the parliamentary election.

JP died on October 8, 1979 at Jaslok Hospital.

JP was engaged in two struggles: one during British rule for Independence and the other during Emergency for Total Independence. The educated people: teachers, lawyers, journalists and the students followed JP, as if he was another Gandhi.

SABARMATI,
January 30, 1930

CHI. JAYAPRAKASH,

I have your letter. I was glad to know that you were able to find work in the Congress office. Now we shall only be able to meet when your work brings us together. If I stay out of jail for any length of time, you must keep writing to me.

Blessings from

BAPU

⊛    ⊛    ⊛

YERAVDA JAIL,
November 21, 1930

CHI. JAYAPRAKASH,

Today I have sent you a telegram about Prabhavati which you will have received. I await your reply. I hope you have sent her to the Ashram. The best thing of course would be for you to go with her and have her fixed up there. Any programme about her future work can be decided after she gets well. I understand your sorrow. I have thought over it. You should not say anything to Prabhavati. If she is moved by desire there will be no problem. But if she has no stirrings of desire, it becomes your duty to protect her.

I need hardly remind you that women have as much right to freedom as men. It is my firm opinion that if one partner in marriage has sexual urge it is by no means the duty of the other partner also to have such urge, though it is the right of the partner with the sexual urge to satisfy that urge. This is perhaps one of the causes of polygamy. Just as it will be considered immoral for a man to cohabit with a wife who is ill it should also be considered immoral to cohabit with a wife who has no sexual desire. It is therefore my earnest advice that if Prabhavati has no craving for sex you should give her freedom and find yourself another wife. I see no immorality in that. After all what is to be done? How can your craving be forcibly stifled? You consider sex necessary and beneficial for the spirit. In such a situation I would not consider a second marriage immoral from any point of view. In fact, I feel that your doing so may well set an example to others. Many young men use force with their wives. Others visit prostitutes. Still others indulge in even worse practices. Prabhavati has chosen to live the life of a virgin. You do not wish to practise *brahmacharya*. Therefore, I see nothing wrong in your respecting the wishes of Prabhavati and finding yourself another wife. If you cannot think of another woman, you should, for the sake of Prabhavati, observe *brahmacharya*.

Blessings from

BAPU

November 27, 1930

CHI. JAYAPRAKASH,

When I think of Prabhavati I feel that the sooner she goes to the Ashram the better it will be. That she will go to the Ashram if she does not recover will mean that she will go when her illness has become worse. You who have been educated in the West should understand that illness should be tackled at its inception. I have known cases of hysteria where recovery was effected by the transfer of the patient to a different place. In Prabhavati's case, it is doubly necessary that she should have a change of weather. She is ailing and she is also faced with a moral crisis. In a freer atmosphere, she will be better able to know her heart and she will also discover her duty. The difficult question before you is that of freedom of women. If Prabhavati has as much freedom as you, you must concede to her the right to think for herself.

Blessings from

BAPU

December 11, 1930

CHI. JAYAPRAKASH,

I have your beautiful letter. What you have thought about Father is only right. I shall say nothing more about it. I hope you were successful with Ghanshyamdas.

As regards the motherland being considered as your mother there is a flaw in your thought. Just as loving one's mother does not mean that one should not love another's mother, so also loving one's motherland does not mean hating other countries. Where there is no love for the motherland love of the world is an illusion. And since the motherland has a greater right over us, being proud of the motherland without any ill will for other countries is only proper. I cannot directly care for the children of the whole world. But if I care lovingly for the children who are in my keeping I shall to that extent be doing service to the children of the world. The case of the motherland is exactly similar. After all it does matter in which land and in which atmosphere we are born. Ahimsa has its origin in this thought. In so far as ahimsa means universal love it can have direct application in our serving the creatures who are nearest us.

I hope you will now take Prabhavati to the Ashram.

Blessings from

BAPU

CHI. JAYAPRAKASH,

I have your letter. I had already decided that Prabhavati should go. I like your decision. If Prabhavati is not deceiving herself it would appear that she is free from desire. Even when she is with you she has no sexual urge and only becomes ill. I therefore think that you should free her. Doctor Jivraj also examined her. He too advises that if she finds it difficult to keep up marital relations she should be allowed to abstain. If you do this it will not be necessary for you to pay her monthly expenses. I would like you to send her to me as soon as possible.

I have had a talk with Ghanshyamdasji about you. This is not the occasion to go to him. It will be good if you can come and see me once.

Blessings from

BAPU

CHI. JAYAPRAKASH,

I received your letter just now at 10 p. m. There has been a misunderstanding. While you are in Patna the expenses will be negligible. My impression was that you ate at the camp. Your going to Bombay has already been arranged. As to your programme after you are relieved of the Delhi work, I had asked you but you refused to say anything. Prabhavati also was not in a position to tell me clearly. I want to make a villager of you. But today you do not have the necessary strength. Since you want me to have the onus of deciding the matter I shall fix Rs. 20 or Rs. 25 per month to be paid to you. Many co-workers are paid less. I shall allow the same sum for Prabhavati. I would want Prabhavati to live at Wardha. The three of us had agreed on this. If now you feel differently Prabhavati will have no objection if you can let me know what she will be doing in Bihar or anywhere else. It is also not clear to me whether you wish to have her with you or just anywhere in Bihar. All this is very delicate. I do not wish to interfere in any way. When both of you need my advice I like it because I feel that I can share your life. But I would like it more if you could each conduct your life according to the wishes of the other. Only yesterday I was ready to send Prabhavati to you. But she does not wish to go in this way. Madanmohan says you will be going to Madras on the 17th. Prabha says: "What would be the use of my going? Jayaprakash cannot even spare a minute to talk to me." I do not like all this. I want something definite from both sides. I shall be reaching Bombay on the 24th. I suggest that you come there. Talk to Prabha and let me know your joint decision.

I have talked at length with Masani on communism. I have read your syllabus. I do not like the manifesto that has been issued. I have pointed out its blemishes to Masani. I shall also speak to him when I can spare the time.

Blessings from

BAPU

July 20, 1934

CHI. JAYAPRAKASH,

I have your letter. It is clear. I now understand your situation clearly. It is natural for you to wish to have Prabhavati with you. Such being the case I do not wish to keep her at Wardha. I am certain that Prabhavati can do some work in Bihar. But Prabhavati does not have that feeling. She has not enough self-confidence. If she could be pursuaded of the virtue of going to Bihar, it would be well. The way is now clear. You can have Prabha anywhere you want. You should both decide something together. I shall have nothing to say about it. I can only give advice when you seek it.

Yes, I do want that neither of you should coerce the other. The ideals the two of you pursue are different. No doubt I have had a hand in shaping Prabhavati's ideal and I do not regret it. But if your love draws her to your ideal, it will be all right by me. It will lessen my responsibility and give you satisfaction. It is a matter of sorrow to me that your life is becoming dreary. Send for Prabha or come and meet her. Take some decision.

To what extent it is right for you, considering your communist beliefs, to accept help from me I cannot say. I cannot also say where we disagree and why. We shall argue about it.

Blessings from

BAPU

September 14, 1934

CHI. JAYAPRAKASH,

I have your telegram. Prabhavati is going but not happily. She has decided that she will cheer you up and come away again soon. When your first telegram came I told her that she should go at once. But she did not agree and wrote to you. She waited a long time for your answer, but there was no answer to the very last moment. Then when your telegram to me arrived, I decided that it was my duty to persuade Prabha to go.

Prabha's difficulty is that she made a promise to Mirabehn that she would do the work that Mirabehn did till the latter returned. Later Ba also went away after extracting another promise from Prabha—for she knew about your telegram. Prabha told Ba that she could go and promised her that she would not leave till Ba returned. Still, since the work consisted of serving me I told Prabha not to worry about me but go. She is a little troubled as she goes.

Another thing is that you have both decided that Prabha should serve in the Kanya Ashram for five years. She should not get out of this. It is as well that she has not yet taken up this work. But how can she give it up?

However, concerning all these matters I am neutral. I have no right to come between you two. I only regret that the education that Prabha has got from me does not have your entire approval. But that education cannot go waste. What she has assimilated is now part of her. You can now strike at her heart as many blows as you like. I have told Prabha not to pay any heed to my advice but to do as her heart and her reasoning dictate.

I have your sweet and pure-hearted letter. Since I was hoping that you would be coming here I did not answer it. I am conscious of the regard and esteem in which you hold me. We shall talk when we meet.

My commitment for paying you stands. I have made an arrangement about it with Ghanshyamdasji too. It was you who had raised the question of moral dilemma. It is you who must take a decision. We shall do as you say.

I hope you are in good health.

Blessings from

BAPU

[March 12, 1936]

CHI. JAYAPRAKASH,

I read your book carefully and liked it although the attack on me which it carries betrays considerable ignorance regarding me. That can be removed but I am enchanted with your study. After these preliminaries I may say that I find in it no remedy for our problem. Your solution does not suit the conditions in this country at least for the present. The goal you aim at is almost the same as that desired by me and many Congressmen. But our method of attaining it differs from yours. Your method in my opinion is not practicable in this country. I am not so attached to my own method that I cannot see the merits of anyone else's. But I am unable to appreciate your solution in spite of all sincere effort.

Your speech at the Bengal session had been travelling with me and I read it only today. I like your resolution regarding the committee of experts. Have you anyone in mind who can do justice to the work? Have you taken any further step in this respect? Your book has given rise to many thoughts with more to come but I cannot write anything just now on that topic. Prabha writes that you are totally negligent of your health; this is not good.

Blessings from

BAPU

SEGAON, WARDHA,
March 17, 1941

CHI. JAYAPRAKASH,

I have your letter. Yes, I saw your statement. I have objections about it. It seems to confirm what appeared in the newspapers. That is the impression it has left on Rajendra Babu also. When you saw me last you had appeared to be satisfied. Rajendra Babu says that your statement confirms the impression he had formed of it from the newspaper reports. If that is so there is nothing I can say. I have the feeling that your statement disguises your views. I have great regard for you and it is my dream that you will do great service to the country. Reading your statement therefore distressed me. It is not proper for a true public servant not to do what is his obvious duty. Look at your last sentence: "The reason why we want covertly to change the direction of the movement is silly." Everything silly is not necessarily untruthful. I understand about covert ways but being in a movement I would consider it improper to seek new directions.

But all this is my impression from reading your statement. If it is not correct then I have nothing to say and I will trust your word.

Now about your health. I am confident that if your adopt the treatment I have prescribed you will fully recover. For the first four days you must live entirely on orange juice. You can have anything up to 16 oranges. During this period and afterwards, at 2 or 3 p.m. when the stomach is empty, you should sit in a tub of cold water. In the Kuhne tub the legs remain outside. You should then rub the part of the stomach that is in water gently with a small towel. You may remain in the tub for half an hour. In the morning after the toilet you should have the whole body massaged. For this you may use the services of my friend who may be with you or any worker that may be given you. You should instruct him in this work. You yourself should be conversant with it. The way to instruct him is to give him a massage yourself. The oil may be any kind; coconut oil or mustard oil will be quite good. You should mix a little camphor in it. Make the camphor into powder and then mix it in the oil. On heating the camphor melts and mixes better with the oil. One pound of oil will require an ounce of camphor. Practise sitting straight in open air for twenty-five minutes and doing breathing exercises. This is necessary to regulate breathing. After the massage wash yourself with hot water. In washing use a small towel to rub the body.

Your food should consist, the one month, of raw and cooked vegetables and oranges. Boil eight ounces of vegetables and drink the soup. Take a quarter of the roughage that is left. But if you feel hungry you may take all of it. You should take 40 grains of soda bicarb daily. It may be added to the vegetables and to the orange juice. The vegetables may include carrots, turnips, radishes, and leaves such as spinach, mustard, shoots of pea, lettuce, celery and radish leaves. These should be eaten raw as also carrots. Or they may be crushed and their juice extracted. You should take two ounces of raw vegetable and six ounces of carrots, etc. The quantity may be modified. You should have clear motions. If there is any difficulty you should take enema and if that does not work take half an ounce of castor oil.

Every day you should consume altogether five pounds of liquid. In the morning take hot water with honey or glucose. Clean your nose every day by taking hot water through both nostrils and bring out the water from the mouth. After this you should drink four ounces or more of hot water through the nose. Go for a walk daily according to your strength.

In the jail your first duty is to build up your body, forgetting the world outside. That is what I call satyagrahi jail.

Blessings from

BAPU

February 17, 1942

I had your letter. The last three lines had been struck off. I have conveyed all the answers to Prabha. Even then I am giving here the answers to your questions. There is no danger in practising *pranayama* Western style. Breathe slowly through the nose in and out sitting erect or standing in the open air. Doing it on an empty stomach daily morning and evening will make you feel better.

Your giddiness must go with hip-baths. Many people have been cured thus.

Eat raw lettuce, radish, carrot and onion with your meals. Take garlic also, not more than one tola, with curds or with cooked vegetables. I prefer castor oil in small quantity instead of liquid paraffin.

Blessings from

BAPU

CHI. JAYAPRAKASH,

I feel that today you are the God in Bihar. Will Bihar really become calm? We have committed a grievous error. Write to me frankly what is likely to happen now. Give me your unreserved opinion. I have a feeling that there should be no Congress [session] this time. Leaders of all the provinces should remain in their own provinces. You may convey my opinion to all. I may not be able to do it as I have little free time.

Where is Prabha ? What does she do?

I hope you are keeping well.

Blessings from

BAPU

SHRI JAYAPRAKASH NARAYAN
PATNA

☐

# Letters to Prabhavati

CHI. PRABHA,

I trust you get my letters regularly. The last of your letters
was from Sitab Diyara. I have received the book written
by Jayaprakash and have been reading it. Tell him that
I shall send him my opinion after finishing the reading. It is
exceedingly cold today and it is windy. Dr. Ansari examined
me today. The blood-pressure was 156/94, but last evening
it was higher. The doctor, therefore, thinks that I should
still be moderate in work and observe the restrictions.
It is very good that at Sitab Diyara you get milk [from the
cow] at home. You should increase the quantity as much
as you can.
Blessings from
BAPU

CHI. PRABHA,

I have had no letters from you of late. I wrote to you a brief
note yesterday. I write this letter today as I wish to send the
letter I have written to Jayaprakash on his book. Perhaps
you are both at Allahabad by now. Jamnalalji, for his
part,has already gone there. Rajen Babu too was there.

Jayaprakash's book is worthy of your reading and
observation. Some of his ideas are wrong, if mine are right.
Is a person great just because all want to follow him?
Rajkumari is expected to arrive today.

Blessings from

BAPU

□

# Letters to Dr Rajendra Prasad

Dr. Rajendra Prasad imbibed and symbolised the three; Simplicity, Spontaneity and Humility. He was sincere, devoted, patient, truthful and determined also. He grew from strength to strength, and helped others to grow. The nation adored him during life time and still shows respect decades after his departure. In fact, India is devoted to moral values, inner qualities and power, and knowledge and wisdom. Dr. Rajendra Prasad possessed and represented all these qualities.

Dr. Rajendra Prasad was born at Jeeradei in the Saran District of Bihar on 3rd September, 1884. He was the youngest child of Mahadeva Sahay and Kamaleshwari Devi. His primary education was completed at home under a Maulavi. He studied at R.K. Ghosh Academy, Patna and Hathua High School. He was admitted to Presidency College of Kolkata in 1902 and came out with a Law Degree in 1915. He got his doctorate degree in Law from there and started practice at Patna High Court. He was married to Rajbanshi Devi at an early age of 12.

On his way to Champaran, Gandhiji stayed for a night in Patna at his residence. When he started 'Champaran Satyagrah Andolan,' Dr. Rajendra Prasad joined hands and prepared all the papers to be submitted to the British Government. They tasted the first victory when their demands were accepted and Indigo cultivation was abolished.

In 1920, he joined Congress and worked as its President for three terms: 1934, 1939 and 1947-48. He established National College at Patna in 1921. During Salt Satyagrah, he arranged and led groups for preparing salt. In 1934 earthquake, he collected four times greater money than the Viceroy and helped Bihar come out of the heavy destruction.

In 1946, he presided over the Constituent Assembly. He wrote many books, *Champaran Mein Satyagrah*, 1922; *Bharat Ka Bibhajn*, 1946; *Atma-Katha*, 1946; *Mahatma Gandhi Aur Bihar*, 1949; *Kuchha Smritiyan*, 1949; and *Bapu Ke Kadamo Mein*, 1954. The Constitution of India was adopted on January 26, 1950. He was elected the first President of India and retired in September 1962. He lived at Sadaquat Ashram, Patna and departed from the world on February 28,1963.

Dr. Rajendra Prasad lived with one aim: service to the nation. He followed his conscience and Mahatma Gandhi. His only path was the non-violence taught by Gandhi. He maintained simplicity in clothes, deeds, ideas, words and life-style. He was known for simplicity which remained the mark of his identification throughout his life.

ॐ

SABARMATI,
August 17, 1929

BHAI RAJENDRABABU,

I have a distressing letter from Krishnadas. I enclose a copy of it. I have written fully to Ram Binod. I am also enclosing a copy of my letter. If he does not want to compromise then the matter will have to be taken to court. I believe you will be coming here on the 21st. We shall then talk more. I shall inform you when I get Ram Binod's letter.

BAPU

BHAI RAJENDRA BABU,

I have your letter. A short preface is enclosed herewith. You may send it if you like it.

I hope you are fully recovered by now.

I shall be in Poona on the 28th and expect to reach Sevagram by the 6th or the 7th August.

What happened to the Urdu book?

Blessings from

BAPU

DATTAPARA,
November 12, 1946

BHAI RAJENDRA BABU,

You have again fallen ill ! How are you now? What is the condition in Bihar? Are those who committed the atrocities relenting? Do they need me there? They should not. If the Bihar fury does not abate, I do not wish to remain alive because my life would then be meaningless. Write to me what precisely the condition is.

The work here is very delicate. Let us see what comes about.

Blessings from

BAPU

DR. RAJENDRA PRASAD
PATNA

□

# A Letter to J.B. Kripalani

J.B. Kripalani was a professor at L.S. College, Muzaffarpur. When Gandhi was on the way to his maiden visit to Champaran, he informed Kripalani and wished to meet him at the station.

During the night when the train reached Muzaffarpur Junction, there were myriads of people to welcome Gandhi. He broke his journey, stayed there and had many meetings with the lawyers. He got all the needed information that Raj Kumar Shukla was unable to give.

Later on, Kripalani became the Prinicipal of Gujarat Vidyapeeth (from 1920-27). He worked as the General Secretary of the Indian National Congress from 1934 to 1945. He was elected its President in 1946 but resigned in 1947. He was a member of the Constituent Assembly. He resigned from the Congress in 1951.

His wife Sucheta Kripalani was also a very famous political figure and associate of Mahatma Gandhi.

His wife Sucheta Kripalani was born in 1886 and died in 1962.

৪০৫৪

KAZIRKHIL, RAMGANJ P.S.,
NOAKHALI DISTT.,
February 24, 1947

This is a very personal letter but not private.
Manu Gandhi, my grand-daughter as we consider blood

relations, shares the bed with me, strictly as my very blood...
as part of what might be my last *yajna*. This has cost me
dearest associates, i.e., Vallabhbhai, Kishorelal, probably
C.R. and others. This includes Devdas. I have lost caste
with them. You as one of the dearest and earliest comrades,
certainly before Sardar and Kishorelal, should reconsider
your position in the light of what they have to say. Perhaps
Sucheta will help you somewhat. She knows something
of this episode. Am I worthy of the companionship of so
many old associates? I have given the deepest thought to
the matter. The whole world may forsake me but I dare not
leave what I hold is the truth for me. It may be a delusion
and a snare. If so, I must realise it myself. I have risked
perdition before now. Let this be the reality if it has to be.

I need not argue the point. I have simply conveyed the
intensity of my thoughts.

I suggest your discussing with Sardar and Rajaji. And then
come to the conclusion and let me know. You have to think
out your relationship not merely as a friend but as President.
Of course you can share this with Jawaharlal and Maulana.
Do not consider my feelings in the matter. I have none. All
I want is to *do* the truth at all cost, as I see it.

Blessings from

BAPU

## Missing

Let me give you some good news too. Today some League
friends met me and expressed their wish to live with the
Hindus amicably and wanted the Government to listen to
them. I said to them that though the League represented a
large number of Muslims I did not agree that those who were
outside the League were not Muslims or that the League was
the sole representative of the Muslims. The boycott of the
League would not do. I even asked the Noakhali Muslims
to obey the orders of the League. So long as they were in
the League, it was their duty to carry out its orders. But

if the League misguided them and asked them to slit the throats of the Hindus, they should refuse to obey it and quit the League.

The League friends also said: "Though we belong to the League still we are friends of the Hindus. If the Government does not take us into confidence, how can the Muslims trust it? If we plead with the Muslims who had run away, they will come back. But if we do not co-operate how many Muslims can you bring back? Maybe a few of them would return. But all of them will not . The Government should consult us." I told them it was a good and straightforward suggestion. Each should co-operate with the other and do his duty. When we work unitedly it will have its impact on India as well as on the world. It will purify our hearts. We should act only with a pure heart. What is the use of our being together without unity of hearts?

I also heard some Muslims say that there were ten crore Muslims and even if one crore perished the remaining nine crores would fight for founding a nation of their own. I told them that if they had such notions they would not serve Islam in any way. On the contrary they would destroy it. I had told the Hindus also in Noakhali that they should get rid of all fear. We should fear God alone. It is cowardice to agree to something or to bow our heads before others out of fear.

The friend from Noakhali has informed me that after my return from Noakhali the situation there has deteriorated again. I told him that if the Hindus in Bihar co-operated with me, I could work for Noakhali while I was still here. I would appeal to the Muslims of Noakhali, if my voice could reach them, to live in unity with Hindus, wherever they may be. Hindus should do likewise. I do not know what will happen in Noakhali in future—whether the surviving Hindus will be killed, their houses looted or burnt. But if this happens, the Muslims will dig their own graves. Even here I hear voices are being raised that scores will be settled once Gandhi goes away. This is a bad omen. I beseech you not to become cowards, but to be truthful and have faith in God. It is folly to agree to anything out of fear. Today some Domes came to see me. They told me that it was not only caste Hindus who boycotted them but even the Bhangis among Harijans boycotted them. They said that the Domes were normally engaged in bamboo work, only the poor ones did scavenging. They are not even aware of the exact strength of their community. Only one boy from the community goes to college. The Domes invited me to stay with them. I told them that, though I would like it, I was at the moment engaged in other very important work. I was grieved to know that the Bhangis did not allow them to draw water from their wells. Bhangis and other Harijan friends should not discriminate amongst themselves. I fail to understand why others regard Harijans as inferior. I have myself become a Bhangi. If I swept your lanes and cleaned your latrines, and you hurled abuses at me and I tolerated them, how would I then become low? Those who are engaged in scavenging are not inferior but it is those who abuse others that are low. Those who do the cleaning for us and serve us should be treated with love by all of us.

□

# Letters to Kasturba Gandhi

Kasturba Gandhi was a sincere and devoted wife, and a caring and alert mother par excellence. She accompanied and worked with Gandhi and daringly matched the pace. Gandhi accepted:

"I must say I was passionately fond of her. Even at school I used to think of her and the thought of nightfall and our consequent meeting was ever haunting me. Separation was unbearable."

Kasturba was born in 1869 in Porbandar in Kapadia family. They lived very close to the house of Gandhis. It was visible from their terrace. Under very adverse and challenging circumstances, she gave birth to her four sons and fostered them. Once, she went to South Africa when Gandhi (already in South Africa) sent for her.

Gandhi was presented gold watch, diamond ring, gold necklace, gold medal, gold coin and gold chain by various persons and agencies in South Africa, which he handed over to the Indian community but Kasturba never talked about them. She did not say anything when Gandhi cancelled the insurance policy under the moral philosophy of Aprigraha; not even when her son spent a total of 393 days in jails in South Africa for his political activities, as against 188 days in jail by the Mahatma himself. Kasturba herself spent many months in jail there.

When Gandhi came to Champaran and stayed there for long, she followed him and worked for the betterment of living condition and education of the ladies of different areas. Once, she tore off half of her saree and gave it to a poor woman who had nothing to wear.

There was a wonderful understanding and adjustment between the two, and faith and confidence over one another. They were dependent and yet independent. Such a couple is rare and seldom to be found. It is clear with Gandhi's anxiety when she fell ill at Age Khan Palace Prison:

"It is unbecoming of the Government to impose such conditions on a dying woman. Supposing she wants the bed-pan when Dr. Dinshaw Mehta is there, who is to give it to her if the nurses are not to be near her? Supposing I ask the nature cure doctor how my wife is progressing, am I to do so through someone else? This is a curious situation. I would be far, rather the government sent me away to another prison, instead of worrying me with pinpricks at every step. If I am away, my wife would not expect any help from me and I will be spared the agony of being a helpless witness to her suffering." *Kasturba: A* Sushila Nayar: *Personal Reminiscence*

Page-81

ॐ

September 13, 1932

BA,

I have your letter. You have probably heard about my fast. Do not get frightened in the slightest degree by the news and also do not let the other women get frightened. Indeed, you should rejoice that God has granted me an opportunity to go through such an ordeal for the sake of dharma. I also hope that you have understood the meaning of this fast. I shall not have to start the fast if my demands regarding the *Antyajas* are accepted, and even if I have started it I can end it. If, however, I have to carry it on till the end, you should indeed thank God. Only one in millions meets death for which he has prayed. What a good fortune it would be if

I met such a death! And if I do not die, it is clear as daylight that it would then be my moral duty to purify myself still further and to devote myself more to service. I think that after having lived with me for fifty years you will be able clearly to understand this simple thing and willingly follow me.

⊛    ⊛    ⊛

PATNA,
March 20/21, 1934

BA,

I have still not received your letter this time. I am writing this on Tuesday after morning prayer. I am in Patna. By my side is Satisbabu, spinning on the takli. There is Rajendrababu's sister. Prabhavati too. Om and Kisan are preparing to go to bed. Swami also is sitting near me. Mirabehn has gone to get the milk ready. Malaviyaji, Maulana Abul Kalam Azad, Dr. Mahmud, etc., are here just now. There was a meeting of all of them on Sunday. At that meeting a new committee was appointed for relief work in Bihar. Jamnalalji also is a member of it. The work is progressing well. I visited Motihari and other places. Even big mansions have been reduced to heaps of brick and mortar.

Everywhere in the streets we saw heaps of bricks and ruins of buildings. The fields are covered with sand ejected with water from the bowels of the earth. Till this sand is removed, no crops can grow, and removing it is no easy work. For it is not only one or two *bighas* that are so covered. Thousands of *bighas* have been covered and in some places the layers are six inches thick or even thicker. The people's misery, therefore, is beyond measure. But even then life is so dear that people, dizzy with the thought of having escaped death, can forget their hardships and keep smiling faces. They have no food in their homes and no clothes to wear, but they do not seem to worry much about that. Such is the scene here. What can we do to help them? Those who are working in the midst of the people may serve them humbly and unostentatiously. They may plead with the idle to start working, and teach sensualists self-control by their own example. They may teach people *Ramadhun* and turn them Godward. There are such silent workers, too, at many places. God's ways are beyond our understanding. He erased the difference between birth and death in a matter of two minutes. Who was born and who is dead? Whether human beings are born or die, His play goes on. Why then rejoice and grieve? The Lord's name is the only truth. He who is aware of Him and serves Him, that is, His creation, as well as he may, lives. Those who do not do this are as good as dead, though living. Well, having started to write a letter I have given you this week's discourse. There may be a few words which you may not understand. But Dahibehn or Shanta or Lalita, one of them will surely be able to understand them. If, however, there is any word which none of you can understand, ask me its meaning.

After writing the above yesterday, I could not go on further. I have resumed the letter today, Wednesday, in the morning (8.45). I shall soon be called to a meeting. There was another letter from Madhavdas. His health has improved so much that he sees no need now to go to Porbandar. He will remain in Bombay and start some business. Devdas and Lakshmi are quite happy. Rajaji has still not gone to Delhi. Most probably he will come here and meet me before going there.

Blessings to you all from

BAPU

BA,

Don't you feel that you were prompted by God to go there? Moreover Manu also is with you. And so I am not worrying at all. You are a lioness and illness has no terrors for you. Face the situation courageously, therefore. Put your trust in Rama. Ask Manu to write to me every day. Ansari is bound to be there. There is no better doctor than him. Most probably Brijkrishna also is there. And in any case Pyarelal's people are all there.

□